# Boots & Laces

*An insight into women's football in England*

## Acknowledgments

The publishers wish to acknowledge the various clubs for providing information and club histories. The players deserve mention for their cooperation in the compilation of this book. Special thanks go to the FA for supplying valuable material and player profiles for the England team.  Many thanks go to all those people who have contributed articles and information.
Your contributions have been invaluable.

First published 2005
by Sahara Publications Limited
Sahara House, 38 Greyhound Road, London, W6 8NX, England

Copyright © 2005: Sahara Publications Limited, England

Editor: Maysun Butros
Photography by: Gillian Sandford
Design by: Anna Gold

ISBN 1-903022-14-2

# Contents

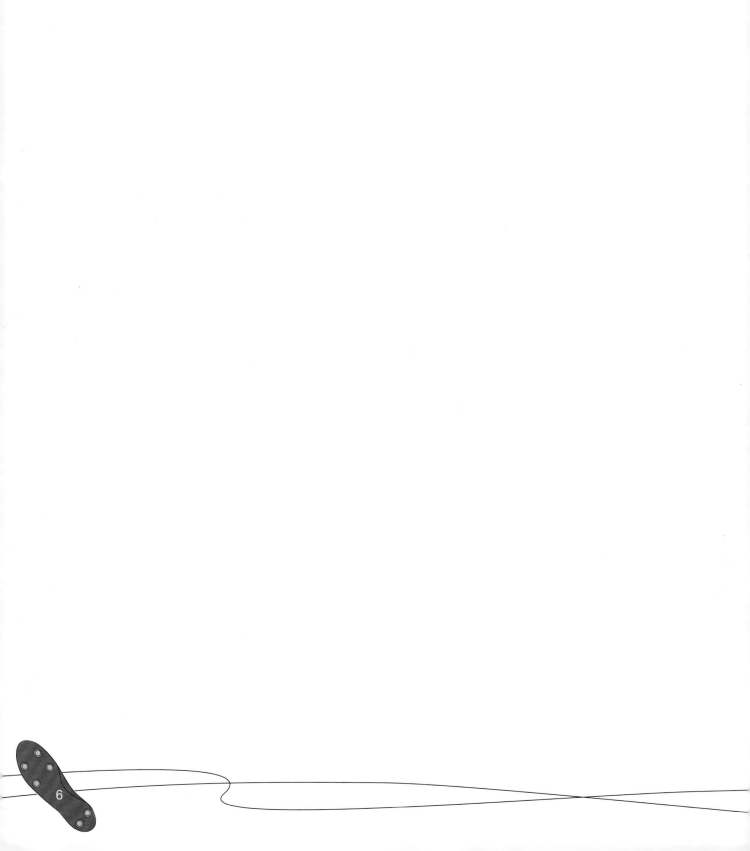

# Foreword

## My Career in Football

I am pleased to be able to write the foreword for this new book on women's football. There has yet to be a comprehensive guide to the clubs and players involved in the game at the top level, so this book just shows how far the game is progressing in this country. I have been involved in the game for over twenty five years now and have seen a definite change in all aspects of the game.

I started my football career playing 5-a-side in the London Union of Youth Clubs League at the age of twelve. It was very forward thinking back then to have had a league for girls. My team then went on to play in the Metropolitan Police 5-a-side competition whose finals were played at Wembley Arena. My local youth club team won through to those finals and we defeated the mighty Millwall Lionesses in the final in front of a crowd of up to one thousand spectators. From this competition I signed for Friends of Fulham LFC, who, in the eighties were vying with Southampton, Doncaster Belles and Millwall Lionesses for the title of best team in the country. Playing for Friends of Fulham LFC was a great period as we had a fantastic squad that played some excellent football.

As the game progressed in the early 90s and the FA took control of the women's game, Friends of Fulham entered talks with Wimbledon FC to become part of the professional men's club. By changing our name to Wimbledon LFC we reaped the benefits of being associated with a professional premiership team. We played our home fixtures at Plough Lane, and we were kitted out exactly as the men in match kit and travel kit and equipment was supplied. Members of the first team and the board including Sam Hamamm would attend our games.

After spending thirteen years with Friends of Fulham and Wimbledon, I decided the time was right for me to move on. Friends of Fulham had been the club side that helped me break into the England squad at the age of seventeen and I had made my debut for them at eighteen. It was a hard decision to make as I had grown up playing football with many of the players at this club and really enjoyed my time with them, but sometimes you have to step out of the comfort zone and challenge yourself to be the best you can. I did this by signing for Arsenal in the season 1994-95. It proved to be the best football decision of my career. Under the managerial guidance of Vic Akers, and playing alongside quality players that were and still are at the club, I became the best player I could.

During the season of 1995-96, I fell pregnant with my daughter Sophie and this obviously changed my lifestyle. Arsenal FC continued to support me, and when I felt the time was right I returned to my playing career with Arsenal, intent on just enjoying club football and doing the best I could. When in 1999 I was recalled into the England squad I was very surprised. I knew I was playing ok but that was possibly because I had no pressure on me as I had achieved everything in the game I possibly could. I had played in a world cup, reaching the quarter final, five European Championships and had amassed seventy six caps to that point. On the domestic front, I had won five League Cup medals, five FA Cup winners medals and four Premier League National Championship medals.

So I made a return to the International scene for the European Championships in 2000-2001. Following this tournament I decided the time was right to retire from the International scene. I also questioned if I wanted to carry on at club level after season 2001-2002. During that season, I played in the UEFA Cup for Arsenal and we were eventually beaten by Toulouse in the quarter finals.

At the end of the season, I was approached by Fulham, who offered me the opportunity to play professionally for one season. It was again, another hard decision to leave Arsenal, but there were other factors around my decision apart from football. Fulham trained five minutes away from my house and ten minutes away from my daughter's school. So I made the switch and signed for Fulham. I consequently ruptured my ACL so only made a few appearances in a Fulham shirt. I am now managing the Fulham Ladies side and feel that my football career has turned full circle. I started at Friends of Fulham and am now managing Fulham LFC.

It is good to see that the game is progressing so well and that respected publishing companies such as Sahara want to get involved with the game and produce a book that all women players and supporters will find an interesting read.

Enjoy the book and keep enjoying the game.


Marieanne Spacey

# History of the Women's Game

*i*t has been a very bumpy ride for women's football since the first recorded match over one hundred years ago in 1895. The women played with hard heavy leather balls, that became heavier when wet, wore long undergarments and hats. But play they did, and have continued to do so ever since, defying attitudes that it was "ungainly, and not very feminine to the eye." During the 1920s, The Dick Kerrs Ladies team played a French team in a charity match in the North of England and a crowd of twenty five thousand watched a convincing English team beat the French 2-0.

Again in the 1920s, attendances reached an amazing fifty three thousand. Unfortunately this was not viewed favourably by the men's game, and a request by the F.A that "all affiliated clubs refuse the use of their grounds for such matches," in effect ended the women's game for the immediate future.

This meant that the hundreds of women all over the country who wanted to play, were relegated to exhibition and charity matches only. However, one of these teams,The Malden Town Ladies was coached by Derek Saville, who impressed by their determination, enthusiasm and skills, encouraged them to keep playing, and by the early fifties they had played hundreds of matches, and raised the considerable sum of over two thousand pounds for charity. They were also endorsed by a small sponsorship! Facilities were non-existent, and a wash down with a bucket of cold water had to suffice after the game. Life after the war years, and on into the 50's

saw a decline in women's football, perhaps due to the pressure of family life, and the return of men into the workplace. It was deemed a man's Saturday afternoon out to watch their favourite men's team play and the women generally stayed at home. However, with England winning the World Cup in 1966, it was hard to keep the women at bay, and teams started to reappear across the country. In 1969 the newly formed 'Women's Football Association' was created with forty four teams, but it wasn't until 1971 when the F.A.lifted its ban on women playing on the grounds of men's affiliated clubs, that the women's game really started to take off again. In 1972 England and Scotland played each other in the first official international game,with England finishing victorious with a 3-2 win.

During the 70's and 80's Southampton WFC were holders of the Women's Football Association Mitre Challenge Trophy a record eight times, with Doncaster Rover Belles reaching the Finals eleven times. To date Arsenal have won the FA Cup six times, and won the treble in 2001.

In 1995, The Football Association Women's Premier League was formed and now consists of the top thirty four teams in the country. These teams are sponsored by commercial ventures, and have access to physiotherapists, nutritionists, professional coaching, and a few **select players are employed full time** in football. A big step forward

Athletic and Arsenal reached fourteen thousand with over 2.5 million televised viewers. On the world stage of women's football, and in America, the World Cup and Olympic Gold medal winners, were the first to be offered full time professional contracts, and their players earn substantial salaries with the added bonus of sponsorship and advertising contracts. The World Cup winning team are household names in America. From Japan to Brazil and South Africa, the women's game is encouraged and is rapidly developing an international platform for women players to show their skills to an ever-increasing field of supporters. This is also reflected in the statistics in England, which prove that by 2002, football had become the top sport for girls and women, and these figures are constantly growing. By 2004 over one hundred thousand players were registered with the Football Association. The England team have been set a target of winning the World Cup in 2007, and Coach Hope Powell believes the team can achieve this. It is a squad built of determined and confident young women, led by Faye White, a tall, strong, and very experienced defender. She led her team to a convincing win against Italy in early 2005, with stunning displays of skill by the whole team in front of a sell-out crowd. The experience of the forthcoming European Championships in June 2005 to be held in the North of England, often said to be the home of English football, should enable them to show the world just how far the England team have progressed over the last few years, and display the new and younger talent progressing through the ranks from club level. The European Championships are the biggest tournament ever staged in England, and the media coverage is substantial, with Sky Eurosport covering every game and the Football Association publicising the games at every opportunity. The achievement of women's football in today's arena, has been generated by the sheer determination of women to compete and play football against all odds, and to ensure that their skills on the field are recognised and respected. The women who play today are creating the future for generations to come, and although there may be a long road to match the crowd attendances and player salaries of the men's game, the women have forged ahead in recent years, and have moved mountains since the days of washing down in cold water after the game.

came in June 1998 when Hope Powell O.B.E. was named as the first ever full time coach for the England squad. She now oversees the U19's, U17's, and U15's together with the senior team, and takes an active part in all areas of coaching and scouting. Since then the women's game has grown in strength and popularity. Girls from the age of six can join girls teams up and down the country and enjoy the benefits of leagues, cup games, management support and encouragement in many areas. The Football Association has established Coaching Schools and Academies with professional coaches and access to first class facilities. The aim is to help and encourage girls to play from grassroots through to the international stage, and to study at the same time. The National Player Development Centre at Loughborough University was opened in 2001 under the guidance of England Manager Hope Powell. Here the top young players in the country can live in, study for sports exams and, with the best facilities available to them at all times. More and more clubs are now affiliated to Universities that can lend their and support to their younger players.

In 2003 The Football Association secured live television coverage with the BBC for the women's FA Cup Final for the next four years. Attendance at last years FA Cup Final between Charlton

# The Football Association

## Women's Football

Women's football has been played in England for over one hundred years. The first match recorded was in 1895 held between a northern and southern team on March 23rd. The North won the game 7-1. Its popularity continued to grow and the early 20th Century was a big era for women's football where crowds of up to fifty thousand watched teams play matches to raise money for charity. Unfortunately The Football Association banned the women from playing on league grounds in 1921 and this effectively destroyed the game in this country for over forty years. When the England men's team won the World Cup in 1966, football mania swept the country and resurgence in the game began. From 1969 to 1993 the Women's Football Association set up and ran a successful England team, a national league, an F.A. Cup competition all on limited funds, but it was very hard for them to develop the game further at grass roots level. In 1993 The F.A. took control.

With The F.A. taking over the game, women's football received a major boost in terms of access to funding and resources. An example of this is in 1993 there were only eighty girls teams, today there are over six thousand teams and in excess of one hundred thousand girls and women regularly playing competitive 11-a-side football.

### League Structure of Women's Football

The Women's Pyramid of Football is the League System for women's football in England, allowing the promotion and relegation of teams from the 'top' of the game (FA Women's Premier League) to the base (County Women's Leagues).

**The Pyramid consists of four levels:**

- The FA Women's Premier League which is divided into the National Division (ten teams), Northern Division (twelve teams) and Southern Division (twelve teams)

- Four Women's Combination Leagues - South East, South West, Midlands and Northern (twelve teams in each)

- Ten Women's Regional Leagues - South East, Southern, South West, Greater London, Eastern, East Midlands, West Midlands, North West, Yorkshire & Humberside and Northern. Each of these Regional Leagues offers a number of divisions and caters for up to seventy teams.

- County Leagues - there are currently ten County Leagues across the country with plans to develop more in the future

## The F.A. Nationwide Women's Premier League

The pinnacle of the pyramid is the FA Nationwide Women's Premier League. Thirty four teams compete in three divisions: National (the top ten teams), Northern and Southern (twelve teams in each on an equal footing, feeding one team each into the National Division every season). The National Division attracts the most publicity. Arsenal, Charlton Athletic and Doncaster Belles have led the way in previous years but now teams such as Birmingham and Everton are realising the potential benefits to their clubs. Arsenal hold the record for a league game attendance, having attracted a crowd of over five thousand to their title clinching game against Fulham played at Highbury in May 2004. The league received its first sponsor in 1998 when AXA became title holders. That deal came to an end in July 2002 when the Nationwide Building Society took over as title sponsors. A National League began under the auspices of the Women's Football Association in 1991 with twenty four clubs. The current holders of the National Division championship are Arsenal, while Liverpool and Bristol City won the Northern and Southern Division titles respectively in 2004.

## The F.A. Nationwide Premier League Cup

The Premier League Cup has been running for twelve seasons since The F.A. took over the running of women's football and is only available to members of the FA Women's Premier League (the National Division, Northern Division and Southern Division). Arsenal have been the dominant team in this competition, winning the cup an impressive seven times.

The 2004-05 season saw Arsenal yet again lift the trophy after beating Charlton Athletic 3-0 at Brentford FC in front of a lively crowd with the match also shown live on SKY television.

## The F.A. Women's Cup

The first ever women's cup began in the 1970-71 season and was called the Women's Football Association Mitre Challenge Trophy. The seventy one entrants were placed in eight geographical groups including teams from Scotland and Wales. Southampton WFC met the Scottish side Stewarton and Thistle in the final played at London's Crystal Palace sports arena on the 9th of May. The inaugural men's cup final was played at the Kennington Oval nearly one hundred years earlier in 1872. Southampton WFC won the game 4-1 with a hatrick from Pat Davies and a goal from Dot Cassell. There was very little media coverage of the historic occasion but the foundations were laid. Southampton WFC went on from this early victory to become the most successful team in the competition, winning the title eight times in the 70s and 80s. The Doncaster Belles have competed in the finals a record eleven times, winning six, but Arsenal have been the most successful recently, winning three of the last five. The FA Competitions Department took over the running of the cup in the 1993-94 season with one hundred and forty seven clubs entering. The competition was renamed the FA Women's Challenge Cup.

Doncaster Belles beat Knowsley United 1-0 in the final. In May 2001 a record attendance of 13,824 turned out at Crystal Palace FC to see a London derby between Arsenal and Fulham. Fulham went down 1-0 to an Angie Banks goal, as Arsenal collected their second trophy in a phenomenal treble-winning season. The 2001-02 final saw Fulham once again competing, but this time against Doncaster Belles, traditionally giants in the women's game. Belles knocked out the holders en route to the final, which was again being played at Crystal Palace FC, but lost 2-1 on another historic day - with two and a half million viewers watching live for the first time on BBC1. The 2004-05 final will be contested by Charlton

Athletic and Everton with the match once again to be broadcast live on BBC1. This showpiece final will draw the 2004-05 season to a close. The 2004-05 final will be contested by Charlton Athletic and Everton with the match once again to be broadcast live on BBC1. This showpiece final will draw the 2004-05 season to a close.

## Football Development

Since The Football Association took over the running of Women's Football in 1993, massive leaps have been made in laying suitable foundations for the game at grassroots level. Now, not only are there numerous opportunities offering young girls an introduction to the game but there is a whole pathway to the top - so talented girls who start playing mini soccer have a defined route straight up to the pinnacle of the game - playing for England. This is defined through the Player Pathway.

At the introduction stage, there are several routes into football. In September 1999, The FA introduced a new version of football called Mini Soccer for the under-10s to play as a fun introduction to the sport that would help to develop their skills. Mini Soccer is played on smaller pitches with scaled down goal posts and fewer players. It allows for greater involvement in the game, with more touches, dribbles and passes.

In schools, The F.A. is keen to ensure that high standards are maintained at all levels and girls are given opportunities to play. The ESFA now runs competitions for girls at Under-12, Under-14 and Under-16 levels. The FA has also implemented a kitemark scheme called the FA Charter Standard Programme for Schools, aimed at recognising and rewarding schools that meet quality standards of provision in football. To qualify for the FA Charter Standard, a school must offer football within and outside of the curriculum for both boys and girls. Since September 2001, six million pounds has being invested in schools over three years to have a dramatic impact on the quality of football activities in this age group. The FA TOP Sports programme provides football equipment, curriculum resources and teacher training for every primary and special school in England - that's around sixteen schools.

Recently the FA has launched a new one million pound investment in Out of School Hours Learning - setting up after school activities. Over 60% of these activities will target girls.

Girls football is also one of nine key sports being given special funding and focus by Sport England's five-year development programme Active Sports. In conjunction with The FA and lottery funding, eight million pounds is being ploughed into developing the game across the country over the next five years, with County FA partnerships delivering training courses for girls to get involved in playing football, developing clubs and identifying talented girls who can feed into the Centre of Excellence Programme. The funding has enabled the County FAs and partners to employ full-time Women's Football Development Officers to run the programme.

Since the launch of the Active Sports Programme there has been a significant growth in youth girls football. There are currently seven thousand affiliated youth teams and this is growing at a rate of one thousand new teams a year-making girls football the number one female sport in England. An example of the popularity of the game came from West Riding County FA who set up a girls league in 2003 with seventy new teams. This has already risen to over one hundred teams.

Active Sports fits within the FA Talent Development Plan for girls football, which provides high quality coaching and support programmes for talented girls. Those aged between ten and sixteen are brought into one of the fifty one Licensed Centres of Excellence across England. Many centres are developing the programme to include sixteen to nineteen year olds in conjunc-

tion with a local Further Education Institute. In London and the South East, the centres play in a weekly fixture programme, ensuring the best possible competition programme. There are plans to extend this nationwide in the next two years.

The pinnacle of the Academy system is the FA National Player Development Centre. Based at Loughborough University and Burleigh College, the Centre provides up to fifteen young women a year with the chance to study on a fully-funded three-year football scholarship. The course is overseen by National Coach Hope Powell and is only available to players with the potential to play international football.

For the most talented girls in the country, The Football Association currently run four England teams - the under 17s, under 19s, under 21s and seniors. In addition there is an under 15 development squad. The under 19s and seniors play qualifiers and finals for European Championships and World Cups.

Both UEFA and FIFA have recognised the FA's Women's Football Development Programme as best practice, and have used the English model in European and world conferences on Women's Football.

## The F.A. National Player Development Centre

The FA National Women's Player Development Centre opened in September 2001 and is a unique venture within women's football as it provides the only football scholarship programme in England that is available exclusively to female footballers. The programme is just part of a structure that aims to put English women's football at the forefront of world competition.

The Scholarship is a partnership between the Football Association and Loughborough Sport. Players are generally aged between sixteen and twenty one and all are full-time students pursuing a wide range of courses in three local academic institutions, Burleigh Sports College, Loughborough College or Loughborough

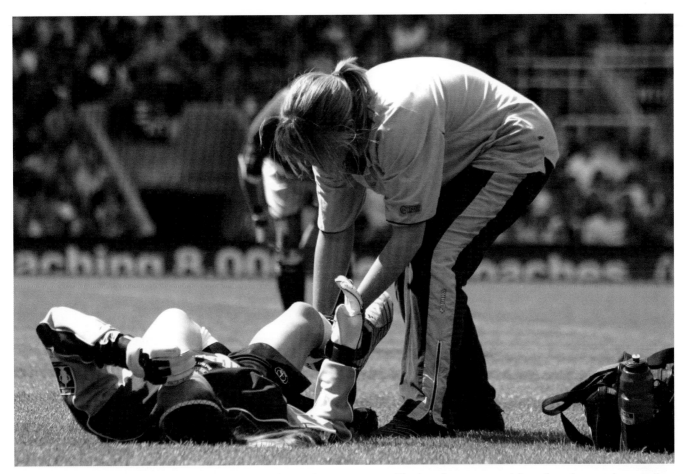

University. They train daily using campus facilities and then play competitively at the weekend for their club.

The Development Programme at the Centre follows the Football Association's four corner player development models with technical, tactical, physiological, psychological and social elements. It is delivered by Football Association staff as well as locally based coaches who are contracted to work with the Centre through the Loughborough Sport Partnership. The environment is player-centred and tailored wherever possible to meet the individual needs of each player.

Loughborough is the ideal place to base the Centre as the quality of the training facilities on campus alone vastly enhances the programme. There is also a wealth of sporting and coaching talent based on the campus which means that in any given week the players don't have to look far for their inspiration. All the girls participating on the scholarship have represented England at some level, either under 17, under 19 or at senior level.

As the National Coach for Women's Football, Hope Powell oversees all aspects of the Centre's programme and is confident that the Centre is pioneering the development of some of the most promising youth international players as well as current full international players.

The players benefit from the expertise from A License coach Jane Ebbage, the Head of the Centre. The girls are also given personal training regimes by FA Exercise and Fitness Scientist Dawn Scott and benefit from medical support from the England Physiotherapist Louise Fawcett and Doctor Pippa Bennett.

## The F.A. Women's Football Awards

The first ever FA Women's Football Awards were held in April 1999 as a celebration of the Women's football season, with eight awards presented. The Awards attracted much media interest and were so successful that it was decided to make them an annual event. The Awards are respected throughout the game because they are voted for either by a panel, players' nominations or by fans of the game. The Awards serve as an excellent finale to a long season and are attended by players from every club in the Premier League along with honoured guests from the game, the media and sponsors.

## Women's football at The Football Association

The Football Association took over the governance of women's football in 1993 and the game has grown tremendously as a result of the resources it now enjoys. Girls' participation in the game has been the real success story, and the excellence programme means that girls now have the opportunity to reach their full potential, through a whole support network.

The Women's Football Committee, chaired by Ray Kiddell, oversees the policy setting across development, international and FA competitions, while the Premier League Management Committee - with includes three divisional representatives - makes decisions on matters referring to the running of the Premier League and Premier League Cup. Peter Hough is The FA Premier League Chairman.

Staff work across all divisions of The FA to develop women's football, from development and international staff to marketing and press office personnel, to running competitions.

As well as those who work specifically on the women's game at The FA, the game is part of Chief Executive Brian Barwick's strategy and therefore a key component of The Football Association's plans.

The women's football committee comprises: Ray Kiddell (Chairman), Peter Hough (vice-Chairman), Mike Armitage, Ray Berridge, Peter Brown, Denis Champion, Tom Farmer, Sylvia Gore MBE, Dave McDermott, Tony Sharples, Paul Simpson, John Ward, Thura Winn.

# The Football Association
## The England Women's Team

**i**n November 1972, the first official international in Britain was played at Greenock in Scotland, with England beating Scotland 3-2. The first goal was scored by Sylvia Gore of Liverpool. England continued to play friendlies away and at home, with the team being run by the Women's Football Association. The Football Association took over the running of the England Women's team in 1993 and Ted Copeland was appointed as the first official team manager. Ted left his role in 1998 and, after a brief spell managed by Dick Bate, Hope Powell became the first ever full-time manager of the England women's teams. In recent seasons the number of spectators attending England games has risen dramatically, with the record crowd actually being doubled in season 2001-02. The England team draws upon players from the Women's Premier League, and Hope Powell

has established a network of scouts across the country to bring talented players into the national set-up. There are now England teams at five age levels, showing the commitment from The F.A. to develop the game at all levels and to give its national women's side the best chance to compete on the world stage.

### Under-15s

Introduced in 2003, the under 15s is a development squad meeting three to four times per year for training. The purpose of this development squad is to identify talented players early in their career and start them on the international pathway. The squad does not play in competition, but provides a good insight into future full internationals.

### Under-17s

Formerly the Under-16s until the 2000-01 season, the Under-17s play friendlies and have training camps because there is no established Under-17s competition at present. At a meeting of national coaches at UEFA headquarters in December 2001, it was agreed that a competition be set-up to give younger girls the experience of playing tournament football. These plans are still progressing. Hope Powell uses the friendlies to assess the talent at this age group and to bring possible future senior internationals into the set-up early to gain the experience of the formation and tactics used by the England team. Each Easter the team competes in an annual Home Nations tournament against Northern Ireland, Scotland and Wales, sometimes with a USA representative side also playing. Jane Ebbage, the Head Coach at the National Player Development Centre, coaches this squad.

### Under-19s

An under-18 squad has been in existence since 1997 when The Football Association identified the need to develop young players at international level. UEFA organised the first Under-18 tournament in 1997, with England reaching the group stages in 1998 and 2000. The team reached the quarter-finals in 1999 and 2001. The youth squad is introduced not only to top coaching, but is also informed on matters of nutrition, strength and all-round fitness. Individual programmes are created for each member. Now renamed the under-19s in line with UEFA and FIFA competition,

the side forges a good link between youth football and the senior England team with several players having made the step-up in recent seasons. A third of the recent Under-19s squad consists of players at the National Player Development Centre - the FA's fully-funded scholarship for female footballers - as well as promising players from Academies across the country. In May 2002, England reached the highest level yet - the Semi-Finals of the UEFA Under-19 European Championship in Sweden, losing 1-0 to Germany, and qualified for the inaugural FIFA under 19s World Championship played in Canada in August, where they reached the Semi-Finals. In 2003 England again reached the Semi-Finals of the UEFA Under-19 European Championship, losing to eventual winners France. It was France who stopped England at the Second Group Qualifying Stage in 2004, but coach Mo Marley's side are hopeful of reaching the 2005 Finals, which will be played in Hungary in July.

### Under-21s

The Under-21 squad was launched in 2004 to bring England into line with several of the leading nations in women's football, who have had a team at this level for a decade. The squad, under the management of Assistant National Women's Coach Brent Hills, competed in their first international tournament in May 2004 - the Nordic Cup, performing admirably against Iceland, Norway, Denmark and Sweden. The squad also played a friendly in Sweden in October 2004, losing 0-1. The squad continues to meet for regular training camps and will play a handful of fixtures each year, bridging the gap between the youth teams and the senior squad.

### Senior Squad

The England Senior team is currently ranked fourteenth in the world and competes in qualifying to reach the UEFA European Women's Championship every four years and the FIFA Women's World Cup, also every four years. England's best performances at this level have been reaching the unofficial European Championship (before UEFA assumed governance of the competition) in 1984, losing over two legs to Sweden. In 1995 England reached the Quarter-Finals of the FIFA Women's World Cup, staged in Norway. England reached the Finals of the last UEFA European Championship in Germany in 2001. With a tough draw, England managed a 1-1 draw with Russia before losing to both Germany and Sweden - who went on to contest the final. England then finished second to European champions Germany in the qualifying round of the 2003 Women's World Cup, meaning they had to go into a play-off. The team beat Iceland in a play-off semi-final, but then lost a two-legged final to France. Staging the UEFA European Women's Championship, in which England have qualified as hosts, has allowed Powell to reinvent the side since the disappointment of not qualifying for USA 2003. Since November 2002 England have played a series of challenging friendlies to prepare for the tournament. This included some tough games against 1999 world champions USA and Canada, with heavy defeats for England showing that new talent was needed. Several youngsters have come into the side since then, with Powell often fielding sides with an average age of 21. The support of FA Partner Nationwide Building Society saw England schedule eight international matches in the first half of 2005 to give Powell's squad the maximum amount of preparation time as they go into the biggest event in their history.

*England captain Faye White*

# The England Team
# Profiles

**Goalkeepers**

**Rachel Brown (Everton)**
Rachel returned to England in January 2003 from the USA to play for Everton and quickly showed her potential, becoming the England number one. Making her comeback after injury, Rachel is looking forward to playing in her native North West during the WOMEN'S EURO 2005.

**Leanne Hall (Fulham)**
A Sheffield Wednesday fan, she played for Wednesday from the age of eleven until joining Doncaster Belles at fifteen. She has since played for Leeds United before moving to Fulham Ladies.

**Karen Bardsley (University of California)**
Karen was invited for a trial in 2003 and successfully gained a call-up to the for the UEFA U19 Women's Championship Finals. A tall, agile keeper, she has featured in the past two England training camps.

**Josephine Fletcher (Birmingham City LFC)**
Another player to progress through u18 ranks and also called into last three senior training camps, she is also waiting to earn first senior cap.

# Defenders

**Faye White (Arsenal)**
In her six seasons at Arsenal Faye won the treble in 2001 and captained the team to The FA Women's Cup and FA Nationwide Premier League double in 2003-04. With thirty eight caps to her name, she has become an experienced member of the squad and captain.

**Rachel Unitt (Everton)**
A full-back or midfield player with a powerful left foot, Rachel broke through to the senior squad at the end of 2000. She won the domestic treble with Fulham in 2002-03 and has thirty six England caps.

**Mary Phillip (Arsenal)**
A versatile player, Mary has played in all four positions at the back and also in midfield. She made her England debut in the same team as current National Coach Hope Powell in 1996. She returned to international action in 2002 after the birth of her two sons. Mary has twenty nine caps.

**Casey Stoney (Charlton Athletic)**
Still only twenty two, Casey has already earned twenty six caps and plenty of winners medals whilst at Arsenal and Charlton. She made her England debut at u18 level alongside Katie Chapman and Rachel Unitt and also wore the captain's armband the last time the two sides met.

**Laura Bassett (Birmingham City)**
Team captain at Birmingham City, Laura was a star performer in central defence for the England u19s, reaching the quarter-finals of the inaugural FIFA u19 World Championship last August She made her senior debut against Italy in February 2003.

**Leanne Champ (Arsenal)**
Leanne was first called-up to the England senior side when she was eighteen years old. Leanne joined Arsenal at the start of the 2001-02 season and quickly made herself the first choice right-back. She has been a key performer for the team in their quest for both domestic and European honours and was again on the winning side in the 2005 Nationwide Premier League Cup Final. She made her England debut in February 2003.

**Anita Asante (Arsenal)**
Anita has recovered from a partial tear of the Anterior Cruciate Ligament earlier this season to play her part in England's WOMEN'S EURO 2005 build-up. Anita can play in defence or midfield and has earned two England caps, both as a substitute against Iceland and Holland in 2004. Rated as one of the most promising up and coming young talents at Arsenal, Anita is also a former Captain of the England u19s. She collected Player of the Year Award in her first full season 2003/04.

**Alex Scott (Birmingham City)**
Alex started her club career at Arsenal, the club she supported as a child, but moved to Birmingham City in the close-season. She has played in attack, midfield and defence. She made her senior debut in September 2004 in the double-header against The Netherlands.

**Becky Easton (Everton LFC)**
Called into seniors in October and November 2004, and then La Manga training camp in January 2005, Becky's last capped appearance with the seniors was against Denmark in August 2001. She featured in the final twenty for EURO 2001 and started against Russia and Sweden.

# Midfielders

**Katie Chapman (Charlton Athletic)**
Katie made her first team debut at fourteen and won the FA Women's Cup and FA Premier League Cup in the same year. She was awarded her first England senior cap at just seventeen. A strong, two footed player, Katie scored her first international goal in a World Cup qualifier away in Holland in March 2002 and has earned thirty two caps.

**Fara Williams (Everton)**
Fara made her senior debut against Portugal at just seventeen years old, coming on as a substitute, and scored a free-kick on her full debut at Fratton Park. She earned over twenty caps at u19 level and has scored five goals in twenty one senior appearances. She won The FA Nationwide Premier League Cup with Charlton in 2004.

**Josanne Potter (Birmingham City)**
Jo plays in left midfield and was a member of the Chesterfield Centre Of Excellence. She started out at Sheffield Wednesday, but soon transferred to Birmingham City, and made an immediate impact by scoring on her debut.

**Vicky Exley (Doncaster Rovers Belles)**
Vicky is a tenacious midfield terrier and possesses one of the most powerful shots in the game. A regular England squad member, she now has thirty nine caps, scoring three goals, the last against Holland in September 2004.

**Kelly McDougall (Everton)**
'Macca' scored on her under 16s international debut and won caps at u19 level before progressing to the senior squad. A regular in the Everton midfield, Kelly made her first senior England start against Russia at Bristol Rovers in August 2004. A full-back or midfield player with a powerful left foot, Rachel broke through to the senior squad at the end of 2000. She won the domestic treble with Fulham in 2002-03 and has thirty six England caps.

**Jody Handley (Everton)**
Jody made her full international debut against Nigeria in a friendly in July 2002 and scored her first international goal for England against Russia in a 2-2 draw in Moscow in October 2003. She likes to play wide on the right, Jody has made fourteen senior appearances.

**Sally Lacey (Birmingham City LFC)**
Sally first played for the England u18s before being called into u21s for their training camp Sept 2004. She was first called into the senior squad for October 2004 training camp and has had subsequent camps in November and January. She is yet to make her senior debut.

**Lindsay Johnson (Everton)**
A pacy midfielder who has two senior caps. Lindsey graduated from the under 21s and has played a key role in Everton's excellent season in The FA Nationwide Premier League and FA Women's Cup. She made the move to Everton from city rivals Liverpool.

**Emily Westwood (Wolverhampton Wanderers)**
Emily is a young midfielder who has played for her country at u16, u19 and u21 level. She is the only player in the squad from outside the Premier League, Emily made her senior debut in the 4-1 victory over Italy at MK Dons in February 2005, playing the entire ninety minutes.

## Strikers

**Amanda Barr (Birmingham City)**
'Munch' scored eleven goals in eighteen games at u18 level and was the Premier League top goalscorer in her first year with Charlton Athletic. She has scored five goals in twenty two senior appearances.

**Ellen Maggs (Birmingham City)**
A diminutive striker who was a key figure as England progressed to the quarter-finals of the inaugural FIFA u19 World Championship. Ellen made her senior debut in May 2003 against Canada and has added three more caps, moving to Birmingham City from Arsenal in the Summer.

**Sue Smith (Leeds United)**
Sue is the most experienced player in the current squad scoring eleven goals in fifty internationals. She signed for Leeds United in 2002 and has twice won the Nationwide International Player of the Year Award. Sue is also a regular on BBC television.

**Rachel Yankey (Birmingham City)**
Rachel scored a wicked free-kick to help Fulham beat Doncaster Belles 2-1 to lift the 2002 Women's FA Cup and was Player of the Match in the 2003 Final. A long-standing and valuable member of the England set-up, Rachel has scored five goals in forty seven appearances for England.

**Kristy Moore (Floya, Norway)**
Kristy was called into the England squad in 2002 after confirmation of her eligibility to play for England. She represented her native Australia in training matches in 1997, but these were not officially recognised by FIFA. She made her debut against Nigeria in 2002 and moved to play club football in Norway in 2003. She is looking for her first goal in an England shirt.

**Eniola Aluko (Charlton Athletic)**
Eniola made her first two senior appearances in the double-header against Holland in September 2004, progressing through the u19 and u21 sides. She made a scoring debut for Birmingham City at the age of fourteen, and now combining studying for A Levels with her football career. Her brother also plays for England u16s.

**Karen Carney (Birmingham City LFC)**
Karen came through England u17 and 19 ranks before first senior call-up to training camp in October 2004. She scored on her senior debut against Italy at MK Dons FC last month and is still eligible for the u19s until the 2005/06 season. She attends The FA National Women's Player Development Centre at Loughborough University

**Lianne Sanderson (Arsenal)**

Lianne scored in all three games in October as the England u19 side qualified for the next round of the UEFA u19 European Championship, earning her a call-up to recent senior training camps. She only turned seventeen in February. Lianne was on the winning side in the 2005 FA Nationwide Premier League Cup win over Charlton Athletic.

England team photos courtesy of FAOPL

# Questions for Hope Powell

*England National First Team Manager*

### What would you say was England's best performance to date?

In six and a half years as England Head Coach it is impossible to single out one individual match. During this period the squad of players and

coaching staff have been building towards a culmination of fitness levels and playing systems to give us the best possible chance of winning games and performing in tournaments, which hopefully we will see this Summer in the North West of England. After every game there are elements of a team performance that you think were good and other parts that need to be worked on. If we had reached our optimum performance, we wouldn't be working collectively as hard as we are to improve our world ranking and be in a position to challenge the best two or three teams in the world.

### Do you think England will ever be able to compete with the dominance of the United States?

As a Coach, one of the things that drives me on is to see England competing at the same level as some of the superpowers of women's football such as Sweden, Germany and the USA. It has been well documented that these countries have invested in elite women's football, almost twenty years ahead of England and other countries, and I am in the business of trying to compete with them. The systems that I have collectively put into place with The FA, including Academies, Centres of Excellence and the National Player Development Centre at Loughborough University, are all geared towards helping English players access the best developmental

support, as well as the introduction of fitness programmes for elite players, which has been another huge step forward in how we prepare our players for the international stage.

### Football in England has moved forward very quickly in the last four years, can you foresee a time when our country will develop Resident Youth Olympic Programmes for young girls in football, or produce youth camps for example?

The system is different in England as we do not compete in the Olympics. The Centres of Excellence as well as the introduction of training camps and youth teams for England from u15 through to u17, u19 and u21 level are all new initiatives in the past three to four years which are all geared to giving young players exposure to international football, different tactics and systems, so that when they make the step up to senior level, they are prepared for the challenges that await them.

### Is a professional league a realistic aim for clubs in England, and if not, why is that?

At the moment you would have to say no, but things can change, and the WOMEN'S EURO 2005 could be a catalyst for this. You only have to look at the men's game to see that a reduction of television revenue has created severe financial hardship for many clubs, likewise the impact that sudden investment can have, and the trauma it leaves behind if the money then disappears just as quickly. At this juncture, The FA Nationwide Women's Premier League is the most competitive I think it has ever been. Whilst the players are mainly semi-professional, which makes balancing a football career and the need to earn a decent wage very difficult, the game needs investment at a level that will support the game for years to come, rather than a short-term fix, if it is to sustain itself.

### Women's football has a friendly and safe atmosphere for families, how would you encourage more people to support the game?

The women's game has taken huge strides forward in the last ten years. Attendances at international level have increased as we try hard to promote the games to clubs, schools and supporters around the country, but with the relatively meagre media coverage the women's game receives, we still struggle to create awareness. A lot of clubs try very hard to promote their teams through community initiatives. For example by sending players into local schools, whilst others get support from the club enabling them to promote forthcoming games on club websites or match programmes. In February, England beat fellow WOMEN'S EURO 2005 finalist Italy 4-1 at Milton Keynes Dons FC. A lot of people, including journalists came for the first time to watch us and went away surprised at the quality of the game they saw. That quality isn't a surprise to me, and I think as new people are attracted to the game, they will come back again as the game has developed so much in the past five years.

### What would your advice be to young female players who may face criticism from peers or parental doubts about the women's game?

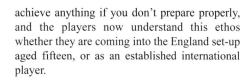

With over one hundred thousand girls and women playing ever week for FA affiliated teams up and down the country, the 'novelty' factor of girls playing football is disappearing all the time I think. Football is now taught within the curriculum at some schools, and there are now seven thousand teams around the country. The emphasis through The FA's Football Development Officers around the country is on getting involved, and then maximising your potential to whatever level, whether it be recreational or going or to play for your country. For parents who have children interested in getting involved in the game, look for FA Charter Standard clubs. These clubs have codes of conduct, a minimum number of FA qualified coaches who have Child Protection and First Aid qualifications, and are geared up to make the introduction to the game fun and enjoyable. There are now over two thousand of these clubs around the country. The friendly against Italy showed how much England have improved recently.

### Have the training, backing and facilities changed in any way?
A large part of the development of the England team has centered around preparation; physical fitness, nutrition and mental preparation. Every player now has a tailored fitness programme from an FA Exercise Scientist and we monitor the players consistently, to ensure that the players are maintaining the programmes we set for them. In the last twelve months we have had access to the players in training camps to build on tactics and team bonding, and with eight warm-up games in the build-up to the WOMEN'S EURO 2005 Championship, we hope to arrive at the tournament at the highest level of physical and mental preparation. If you are in any sport, you can never hope to

achieve anything if you don't prepare properly, and the players now understand this ethos whether they are coming into the England set-up aged fifteen, or as an established international player.

### Who was your inspiration when you were growing up and who encouraged you to keep playing?
I first started playing football as a child playing on the streets with other kids, mainly boys. When I was at Secondary School, aged eleven, one of my friends told me she trained with Millwall Lionesses, and when I went along with her I was amazed so many girls played. When I got home my Mum told me I couldn't play next time, but I snuck out and played, and that was the beginning of my career in football. Throughout childhood it was communicated to me, by family and by coaches, that "you have to work hard to achieve." Players can have all the talent in the world, but you have to work hard, train hard and be dedicated in order to realize your maximum potential, at whatever level that may be.

### What was your most memorable time as a player?
Winning the League and Cup double with Croydon would be my club highlight and at international level it would have to be my first cap against the Republic of Ireland.

### Who is your ideal all round player and why?
In any player I am looking for a combination of five qualities. A player that is technically and tactically astute, has high levels of physical fitness, who is a team player, has good game understanding and who has leadership qualities.

### What is the Coach Mentoring Strategy?
I introduced this in 2001 to support coaches and give them the best opportunity to excel and reach their potential. The scheme is regionalised and coaches are assigned mentors who provide them with feedback and guidance. Once a Coach has reached A License level, we then have a series of practical and theoretical workshops, as well as exposing those coaches to a taste of international football too. Jane Ebbage, Lois Fidler, Julie Chipchase, Julie Callaghan and Mo Marley are all examples of active coaches involved with the England set-up or in the FA Nationwide Premier League who have 'graduated' from this strategy.

# The Football Trust

*By Former MP and Peer Mr Tom Pendry*

*l*et me begin by stating clearly that our vision is one of a united game, a game where there is a common strategy for football, drawing on the good work of the football authorities and the government for the benefit of our national sport at every level. There is a clear need for a much more unified approach to funding, a much greater sharing of good practice and for more opportunities to develop new initiatives. I have opened discussions with the Football Association, the Premier League and Sport England on how best we can achieve this.

One area, which is crying out for such an approach, is grassroots football. By this I mean women's, youth feeder league and parks football. Underpinning the Charter is the FA's National Facilities Plan for Football - an assessment of the facilities required to realise its goals. The FA cannot fund the plan alone, and will rely on county FAs, Sport England and local authorities to implement it. But much more needs to be done for the rest of the game.

*England's Lianne Sanderson*

The more equitable distribution of football's new - found wealth is a major issue in the game. There is money aplenty at the very top of the game but many Football League clubs, both men's and women's, still struggle to survive.There is also compelling evidence that grass roots facilities, at schools and in the parks, are in desperate state of repair and are crying out for investment.Over 70% of organised football takes place on local authority facilities. County FAs are assessing the needs in their area but it is clear that substantial investment will be required to meet the need for small sided pitches and to improve facilities to the required standard. During the late 1980s and early 1990s, due to pressure on local authority finances, many pitches were sold off, and led to the decline of remaining facilities through a combination of over use and under investment. Some 10,000 sports fields, mostly but not all school pitches, have been sold in the last twenty years. Many primary schools in inner cities no longer have access to grass pitches. Is it any wonder our sports people struggle at international level? The Football Trust are the established vehicle for aiding football through grants that bring together government and football in a unique and meaningful partnership.

With the support and continued commitment of our funding partners we can create a long term partnership and strategy for our national game. With television deals reportedly worth £1 billion there are widespread calls for more investment in our game to provide the right facilities for all. It is all very well talking about the football stars of the future, but they need teams to play in and pitches to play on.

To get the best we have to provide for the rest. We are ready to broaden our remit into player development and education and to ensure greater investment in the grass roots, including community based facilities, schools, building links between clubs and communities, supporting inner city schemes, encouraging the development of education centres of football and support for park teams. The Trust can also play a significant role in these areas especially in countering social exclusion. This term encompasses members of our society that have been disadvantaged, and covers a whole range of issues. Personally I think of it as coming down to one core characteristic: alienation. Football can be used as a motivator for those affected. Educational initiatives are springing up at professional clubs and from a purely footballing perspective the following may appear obvious, but nevertheless it is worth pointing out that contact by clubs at this stage may often prove to be an investment in securing the clubs' next generation of players and supporters. Sport impacts on government policies, bringing huge benefit to the country and the community. Football has a role in the economy, the environment and national culture, in health and well-being issues, in combating crime, drug abuse and unsociable behaviour. Football is currently riding the crest of a wave of popularity and has risen from its darkest days of the 1980s to once again truly capture the imagination of the nation. Now is the time to embrace this mood of optimism and create long-term partnership and strategy for our national game.With the continued commitment of our funding partners, the Football Trust will be working flat out to achieve that goal, in the future.

Article reproduced by permission of Christine Oughton, The Football Governance Research Centre, Birkbeck College, University of London.

*Kelly Smith with fans*

# Inside A County F. A.

*By Keely Brown*
*Girls' and Women's Football Development Officer - Derbyshire County Football Association*

*i* was appointed in January 2005 with the specific role of developing Girls' and Women's Football in Derbyshire. My position is supported by Derbyshire Football Association, The Football Foundation and Derbyshire Sport. With regards to girls' and women's football development, the main role of Derbyshire County Football Association Ltd is to provide more opportunities for girls and women to get involved with the sport, either in a playing, coaching or administration capacity. This work extends to supporting and enhancing existing provision of the sport at schools, junior football clubs, Local Authority Sports Development Sections, Football in the Community Schemes and other key deliverers and providers. This process also identifies gaps in provision where new girls' football initiatives can be developed. A priority is to ensure sustainability within the sport and to also ensure that there is always an exit route for those engaged in the sport. This is done by work in the following areas:

## School-club Links

A fundamental theme underpinning all football development is supporting young people to move from school-based football to a suitable club opportunity. Via the three Lions FC programme we help schools and clubs broker sustainable relationships and develop high quality school-club links. There are nine Districts and Boroughs in Derbyshire, and girls' specific school-club programmes will be delivered in six of these during 2005.

## Club Development

It is vital that female clubs and girls sections within clubs have the correct structure in place to accommodate new players from schools and recruitment activities. As a County FA we work with all clubs to gain FA Charter Standard Accreditation. This is an FA initiative that recognises clubs that demonstrate quality in provision, such as meeting required standards, raising standards and reaching excellence. We plan to support six new clubs, either girls only or clubs that have a desire to develop a girls' section to gain this award in 2005. This will be supported by providing subsidised Level 1 Coaching Courses for coaches and assisting player recruitment festivals. Additionally, we will also help other Clubs that require support with Charter Standard applications. At present we have twenty six senior women's teams and thirty two junior girls' teams that are registered to Derbyshire County FA. Over the course of the year and with the interest that the UEFA Women's Championship will generate we hope to see these figures rise.

## Coaching Centre Support

We operate a Coaching Centre that is based at Derby College, Mackworth. This Centre provides the opportunity for clubs and schools to send girls who show potential to receive high quality coaching for twenty or more weeks of the year and the chance to play competitively in East Midland Regional Festivals. Any exceptional players are recommended to the Female Centre of Excellence at Chesterfield FC. At the moment the Centre provides for girls at u12, u14 and u16 level, although for the new season we will be developing an u10s group. These players will be recruited via a series of kick-start coaching courses that will be available around the County and through summer fun coaching days and recruitment activities with Brownie and Guide groups.

port for those clubs in the league that are not already accredited, and also providing support for team development within clubs keen to take on girls' football.

## Inclusion Work

As a County FA we work with other delivery agencies throughout the County to provide football opportunities for girls in deprived wards such as Derby and Chesterfield and for girls from BME and disability groups.

## Promotion and Profile

All of our activities are promoted by producing regular press releases within girls and women's football and are regularly transferred onto our website. We also have an information flyer containing details of opportunities for female players and coaches.

## Centre of Excellence Support

We have one Female Centre of Excellence in Derbyshire that is based in Chesterfield. Ongoing support is provided through promotion and where possible financial contributions to support the Centre and players through festival involvement in conjunction with other teams within the region. We will also be looking to assist the Centre in the Festival around the Euro 2005 events.

## Women's Development

It is also important for us to support and develop opportunities for women to participate in the sport. We will be piloting a women's 5-a-side league that will run from May through to August. This will target ladies teams, business companies and women with families who may have limited time to play for a structured team over the course of a season. At present we do not have a Senior Ladies League in Derbyshire, although this is something that is on our agenda as more teams develop. However we will be looking at the possibility of running a joint County League with Nottingham FA in the interim. Another focus area is for us to recruit more female coaches, and we will be looking to provide coach education bursaries for women wanting to take first-aid, child protection and coaching courses. We also support female mentoring schemes for Level 1 coaches moving to Level 2 status.

## School Development

Our main work within schools is to support all football delivery and to offer assistance and advice where applicable. We again work with schools closely to support their applications to gain FA Charter Standard and by providing more girls' football opportunities. We also co-ordinate the Derbyshire Youth Games (DYG) which involves a girls' football tournament for u10s and u14s. We support District and Borough festivals to ensure that school teams have the opportunity to participate at all districts. In September we will be looking to build on the DYG's and publicity from UEFA Euro 2005 by piloting a school league within one of the School Sport Co-ordination Partnerships. We will also be providing female only Junior Football Organisers courses within secondary schools. A successful JFO was staged at Chellaston School in Derby and a second one is planned for September. This will expand and be offered to other schools and colleges throughout the County.

## League Development

We have a Derbyshire Girls League and work with committee members to ensure that the league provision for girls in the County continues. This again feeds into providing Charter Standard sup-

# Sponsor Ladies Team

## Men's Team to Give Financial Support to Ladies Champions

**a**rsenal Football Club today unveils an exciting and unique new sponsorship initiative that sees the double-winning men's squad providing financial support for the Arsenal Ladies. In the first partnership of its kind, every one of Arsene Wenger's players will be providing funds, which will be used to ensure the continued development and progression of Arsenal Ladies Football Club. Each player will be sponsoring the Ladies player in their respective position, a significant move which gives further backing to the most dominant team in the women's game.

**Arsenal Ladies FC Manager Vic Akers said:**
*"This sponsorship is another step in the right direction for the women's game, and a real testament to the ladies that the support comes from the men's team. Both teams are aware of each other's*

success, with the ladies being arguably the most successful women's team in the history of the domestic game. This additional money will help push the Ladies team forward to what promises to be another successful season."*

**Arsenal Ladies' left back and Development Officer Clare Wheatley said:**
*"I've been a member of the ladies team for eight seasons, in which time we have been very successful. The lads can only continue to raise the profile of our club, as we embark on another season when domestic and European honours will be our goals. As the Ladies' Development Officer I'm also greatly aware of how we need to continue developing the structure of Arsenal Ladies and the women's game in general. Any financial support that we receive will help run our Centre of Excellence and Academy that will hopefully provide the Club with players in years to come."*

**Arsenal FC Captain Patrick Vieira said:**
*"To me Arsenal is about more than just the first-team squad, it is about the football club as a whole and our ladies team is an important part of the club. When I think about last season, of course I think about winning the Premier League and F.A. Cup and the open top bus-ride through Islington. The girls were also there receiving applause for winning their League championship and*

that's how it should be, because their achievements are, like ours, a real credit to this football club."

**Arsenal Goalkeeper David Seaman said:**
*"In the past the goalkeepers in ladies football have come in for more stick than players in any other position, but I've seen how the standard has risen over recent years and our own Emma Byrne is definitely one of the best in women's football. Not surprisingly when Patrick mentioned about sponsoring the girls I opted for my fellow member of the 'Keepers Union'. I've seen Emma in training with Eddie Niedzwiecki a couple of times and have been really impressed and I also saw her make a great penalty save in the women's FA Cup Final a couple of seasons ago."*

**Arsenal left back Ashley Cole said:**
*"I'm a big supporter of the Arsenal Ladies and I think it's a great idea for the lads to sponsor the girls. The ladies don't often play with a conventional left back so the player I'm sponsoring, Clare Wheatley, has a slightly different role for the girls than mine with the men. But there are obviously similarities with us both having responsibilities at the back. Hopefully I'll be able to follow Clare as she enjoys another successful season with Vic's team."*

Arsenal Ladies have representative players as young as eight and upwards at the Arsenal Ladies Football Club Centre of Excellence and Residential Academy. The Club has won honours including five National Premier League titles, seven National League Cups and five Women's F.A. Cup in its history and is looking forward to another season in Europe as the current League Champions.

# The National Player Development Centre

*t*he National Player Development Centre is based at the prestigious Loughborough University, near Leicester. It was opened in September 2001 with the aim of providing scholarships to the country's most talented female players. It consists of first class equipment housing the latest in technology, and the girls have access to astro turf, running tracks and gym facilities that would be the envy of most premier league clubs. The students receive top quality football coaching and training, together with studying for G.C.S.Es, A Levels, NVQ and degrees, in a whole range of subjects. Everything, including all food and accommodation is provided by the Football Association, and overseen by England Coach Hope Powell, who regularly attends meetings and training sessions at the Centre. The girls are all aged between sixteen and twenty-one and the cours-

es run for three years. Their scholarships are reviewed annually and will, in some cases, be awarded over a number of years over the life of the student's academic course

The girls literally can eat, sleep and breathe football without the worry of major financial commitments. They will often train early in the morning and go to lessons throughout the day, and train again in the evenings. Often they will have football coaching sessions between their academic lessons, and at weekends play for their respective clubs. It's a pretty heavy schedule but the girls thrive on it, and the results have proven the system works. When the Centre first opened, Head Coach Jane Ebbage, took the girls under her

wing and provided not only coaching, but also home - college liaison, a shoulder to cry on and general agony aunt. Even now with the amazing growth rate of the Centre, she still finds time to listen to the students and help them to settle in When the new recruits first arrive some of them are only be sixteen years old, and it will probably be the first time they have lived away from home. Jane and Assistant Coach Lois Fidler, are aware of the strains this can impose on the youngsters, and offer a guiding hand when it comes to ensuring that the students make lessons, coaching sessions, gym work, and to remember that meal times etc are also of major importance. The Centre now also employs Sports Phycologist Kate Goodger on a part time basis to help with the day to day care of the girls well being and to offer advice when needed. The Centre also now employs a number of itinerant staff who provide on and off

*Jane Ebbage*

field support in all aspects of the players development programme, leaving Jane and Lois with more time to concentrate on their coaching This new position means that Jane and Lois can concentrate more on football. Both are qualified F.A. Qualified A license coaches level coaches and expect the highest standard of work, both on and off the field.

These students are, after all, the best talent in their age groups within women's football in England, and all play for the top teams. Most who experience the N.P.D.C.style of coaching are expected to make the England Senior Squad at some time. Birmingham City and England player Amanda Barr is coming to the end of her three-year stay at Loughborough, and firmly believes the whole system has made her a better player:

"My confidence has grown and I've learnt so much during my time here, not just about the football but living and sharing with like- minded people, and it has helped me develop into a better player and person. I will be sorry to leave, but it's great to see so many young girls wanting to come here."

Last August the open day attracted over two hundred hopefuls from all over the country, a huge jump from the first invitation-only open day in 2002. As women's football reaches higher levels so will the need to enlarge the number of allocated student places. This demand can only reflect well for the whole of women's football. Jane Ebbage is confident that the stars of tomorrow will benefit from the specialised training and education available to them and provide an outstanding team of players to represent England in the future.

*Lois Fidler*

# My Life in Football

By Keith Boanas
First Team Manager
Charlton Athletic Ladies

*i* first became aware of girls' or women's football whilst coaching in the USA in the nineties. The company I was involved with had us working with local community clubs in the State of Minnesota. All of these clubs involved both a girls and boys programme from under 8s to under 19s, with the girls being the more receptive to soccer as they call it. It was and is recognised as a more popular female sport, right through to senior level. The lads move on to the type set US sports of American/Grid Iron football, baseball and basketball. Anyhow, enough of the US for now. How did I become more involved in the UK? In the mid 90s in my role as a coach educator for the UK, a young lady by the name of Deb Browne attended one of my courses to gain her prelim badge now known as level 2 which she duly passed. At the time she was part of Charlton Athletic Community Programme, and her remit and passion was to develop and promote girls football at a time when ignorance prevailed against it in this country. Women's football existed with the established clubs like the famous 'Donny Belles' and Arsenal Ladies, but organised girls leagues and more seriously developed programmes were few and far between. Deb, with the clubs support overcame a vast number of obstacles to produce a viable plan to gain the required funding and sponsorship to kick start our girls Centre of Excellence. I could not even begin to presume the amount of work and time it took and it would be patronising of me to do so. One evening in 1997, I received a call from Deb to ask if I would consider heading up the centre of excellence as she needed an A license coach. At that time I was predominantly coaching at men's semi-pro level as well as the coach education work. However, it was only one evening a week, and I hap-

pened to be free on that night so I accepted. Close to that time I also became manager of a well known Ryman league side after a successful spell as a player/manager. The centre grew from two age groups to the required four; under 10s, under 12s, under 14s and under 16s, and has evolved into one of the best in the country competing with the other top clubs, and many more joining the programme year by year in organised games and tournaments aimed solely at developing players. This eventually evolved further into our academy for under 16s and upwards, which started humbly at Bexley College, but is now part of London Leisure College, based at the Valley and the Clubs main training ground. At the time of writing I am on a coach going up to Leeds to play their Academy with seventeen of our youngsters, all aspiring to play at the highest level. In fact one member of the group is now an established first 11 squad member and has played for the England under 21s and senior squad, she also won the 2003-2004 Young Player of the Year Award at the National Awards. Ann-Marie Heatherson has progressed from our Centre of Excellence into our Academy, the reserves and first teams, culminating in international recognition. She is living proof that the system can work. To move on, whilst managing the Ryman side, Tooting and Mitcham eventually to a league championship and promotion, as well as my role of centre of excellence and academy director for Charlton, I was also still coaching part time for local amateur teams to help pay the rent. One young lad I was coaching called Kane Brook, just happened to be the nephew of Pauline Cope, who at the time was the England goal keeper and played for Croydon in their double winning team under a manager who should still be involved in top level coaching, Deb Bampten. I was single at the time, having just returned from three months in the US ending a relationship I was in, and on the back of two divorces which my involvement in football had not helped. I met Copey at a presentation night for Kane's team and we clicked straight away with much of the conversation being about football. The rest as they say is history and we have now been together for six years. I want to go into the stupidity and politics of the eventual takeover by Charlton Athletic of the successful Croydon side. Suffice to say that the then Croydon Chairman, instigated the move in the hope that they would gain some financial reward and access

to players from the club for their men's team. When it became apparent that this could not be guaranteed, the mood changed. However, the players had it in their constitution to vote on their own future, this they did and the move followed. Deb Bampten was against it and regrettably resigned. I say regrettably, as I was hoping to work with her as coach. Having not worked with a women's senior side, her experience would

have been invaluable. So a new manager was appointed Gill Wylie, the experienced Irish international and Croydon Captain, became player manager. I accepted the role of coach on the proviso that I would be able to continue my job with Tooting. In the November of that first season, and for everyone involved, the transition was not proving easy, from being an almost social club, albeit successful, to being part of a professional set up was creating problems. The girls were expected to represent the club in a professional manner, without being full time professionals. This caused some rebelliousness and conflicts of interest on how things should be done. The end result of this led to Gill Wylie departing the club along with her Captain, another experienced player Sharon Barber. We had by now recruited a few of our younger players into the squad and so they would now have to make the step up somewhat quicker than anticipated.

I was now approached with a request to manage the team for the remainder of the season, with the help of another veteran of the team who could relate to the players for me, Carol Ozzie Osbourne. Ozzie has since retired, but without her help in those early days, I could not have managed to maintain both jobs. Further trauma was to follow when we ended up losing six key players through disciplinary issues and other reasons. But a rapid re-build saw us end the season in a respectable position and guaranteed us a place in the semi-final of the FA Cup. In the meantime, my Tooting side were also winning the Championship and promotion, gaining me Manager of the Year Award. It had become apparent, that combining jobs was proving extremely difficult and tiring and with a twelve month contract offer on the table from Charlton, I made a very tough decision to leave Tooting and Mitcham and a great set of players. It was one of the toughest decisions I have ever had to make. My remit now was to concentrate on the women's team. I recruited my close friend and A Licensed coach, Kenny Bremner to help, and the process of ensuring we could compete with the best, combining our whole development programme with a successful senior side had begun. With the continued hard work of the new Chief Executive for Women's Football, Deb Browne, and the backing of the CAFC Board in particular Bob Whitehand and Dave Sumners, and the tremendous support shown by Peter Varney and our biggest ally Steve Southerland, I believed we had well and truly arrived. A consistent high league placing, two FA Cup final appearances, a League Cup success and the Community Shield all in a six and a half year lifespan has given us a major boost. Copey is now encouraging more and more youngsters to take up the beautiful game with her drive and enthusiasm in her role as Community Scheme Officer for Girls Grassroots Football. The game for girls is constantly growing and being accepted by all, except the ignorant hard-liners and chauvinists. I have proof that you can walk in both domains and along with many have been converted to the fact that girls can play football. As many before him, our first team fitness and goal keeping coach Mickey Cole was convinced that women's football was not to be taken seriously. Suggest that to him now, I guarantee you would get a rhetorical response, and by that I mean, told where to get off in no uncertain terms. I have certainly enjoyed the experience in the main, apart from a few occasions, where I let the stupidity of one or two individuals get to me. Copey, at the tender age of thirty five is looking to retire soon, so who knows where my future lies. But thanks must go to a great club in Charlton Athletic and every member of staff that I have worked with and most importantly, all the players young and old. Seeing a player you have worked with develop from a young age into international football, is what every coach should want to achieve, not matter what level you work at. Never forget though, the game is there for everyone to enjoy and no matter what level you play at, have fun and do your best. That's all anyone can ask.

# Pauline Cope Skills

As this is being written, Pauline Cope or "Copey" as she is affectionately known, is looking ahead to another FA Cup Final with Charlton Athletic, this time against Everton. Having collected silverware with previous clubs Millwall, Arsenal and Croydon, she says, "the excitement and feeling of a Cup Final never leaves you. If anything it's even better with Charlton where I have spent the last years. We are one of the best teams in the country and the teamwork behind the scenes at this club is brilliant. I'm really happy here and hope to end my playing career whilst at Charlton. After that, who knows? I'd love to coach the England Goalkeepers in the future." Pauline's International career came to an end when she announced her retirement in 2004, but not before amassing an incredible sixty caps for her country, and travelling all over the world, playing against some of the best teams such as Germany and the U.S.A. She takes with her fond memories of her England games, especially playing with two of the greats in English football, Marieanne Spacey and current Captain Faye White. "Marieanne was unstoppable, her desire and strength of her shooting skills was some of the best I have seen in the game, and Faye always leads by example." Pauline is now working for Charlton Athletic's Development Team, encouraging youngsters into the game, providing a sound future for Charlton Athletic Ladies.

**SKILL NUMBER ONE**

1. Balance ball for a few seconds on foot.

2. Kick ball to knee-height

3. Kick ball up and flick leg over the top of the ball.

4. Catch ball with foot, kick up again.

# Coaching in
# the United States

*By Emma Wake*

My first experience of the United States was back in 1992, and I was spending my summer holidays teaching various sports at a small summer camp for girls in Connecticut. I had just completed my second year at university and was spending ten weeks earning some pocket money on the East Coast so I could spend some time on the West Coast. My trip was cut short when I discovered that I had failed one of my second year exams. I remember sobbing on the phone to my mum and yelling:

"There is no way I am coming home."

Of course I went home and I was absolutely heartbroken. I had spent five weeks eating, sleeping, washing, and living in pretty close quarters with twelve fifth graders and it was really upsetting to leave halfway through the summer. Pulling myself away from friends that I had made knowing that they were going to be driving across the States in a few weeks time was agonising. I never really got that out of my system. I did the graduation and I got the proper job and tried the grown-up thing. I never settled and always felt that I had an unfinished project that needed completing. So I returned once again in 1997 in an attempt to get Stateside out of my system. I ended up experiencing what can only be described as one of the best summers of my life. I spent eight weeks at Camp Danbee, in Massachusetts and coached Football -- or should I say soccer. The camp had an intake of around four hundred girls who were generally from wealthy backgrounds. I was coaching five sessions a day in at times pretty high temperatures to girls aged five to fifteen. They ranged in ability - but let's put it this way - the talented were very talented. Generally the athletic kids were extremely gifted and excelled at most sports. A coach's nightmare when a tournament conflict occurred! I spent the rest of the summer travelling around the country , and little did I realise the at I was building a fondness for the U.S that would never settle down again. When I eventually returned to the UK in October, I immediately began planning my next summer. I absolutely loved the idea of coaching girls all day. I remember thinking to myself :

"If only I could coach full time in this country."

I had my contract and visa all sorted out in February. I was going to be a Group Leader ninth grade and coach soccer. All was going to plan . Until my mum fell ill, so ill that I eventually realised that there was no way I could go to America. I was disappointed that I

would not be going but knew that I was needed at home -- and I wanted to be around for my mum. My mum passed away at the end of June. After the funeral I began to feel a little trapped and resented anybody and everybody. My dad eventually suggested that I get away. He thought it would be a good idea for me to go to Camp and take my mind off everything. And that was that. That was the start of my five years in America. I spent the summer at Danbee coaching. During my stay the camp played host to a year round soccer camp where two British female coaches were supervising the young female players. When I discovered that they were on three-year contracts -- I couldn't believe my ears. My immediate thought was:

"Coaching all day -- seven days a week -- I could do that -- my dream job!"

My boss was friends with the owner of the company and managed to arrange an interview for me. I spent the morning at an interview in a park in Montclair, New Jersey and the afternoon playing a game against a high school boy's team. I remember nobody wanting to play left back -- which is pretty common, but I was happy, being all left foot and a full back I jumped at the chance. All I can remember is every time I tackled this tricky forward all the coaches and people on the sideline would laugh and make fun of him. A couple of years later, I saw that same boy represent the United States for the U18 squad. I was offered a job with the company - they wanted to me to start immediately. And that was that -- my career in the U.S had begun for "Ashley's Soccer Soccer Domain." I was based in Montclair, New Jersey and lived with a family in

this unbelievably huge house. I had the top floor --the third floor, pretty much to myself with my own bathroom. At times it was a little scary . I don't think I have ever stayed in a house so big. Montclair is a great place to live in, really diverse, only fifteen minutes from New York City, and everybody is mad about football.

The football season is kind of divided by the four seasons of the year. The Fall season (Autumn for us Brits) lasts from September to the end of November and is viewed by people who do not play footie all year round as the real "soccer" season. The hardcore football kids play all year round. The winter season from November to March becomes an indoor season, due to the snow and freezing temperatures, so teams usually hire indoor facilities,

*Kelly Smith- Wake's choice of best international striker*

either school gyms or state of the art third generation pitches. (Depends how committed, wealthy and accessible each place or team is). The winter season sees teams play a lot of small-sided games and compete in indoor tournaments that are six, seven or eight-aside.

When the spring arrives teams venture outside again and play eleven aside, if they are eleven and older. The season is similar to the autumn but with loads of conflicts such as lacrosse, baseball, and softball. The less serious teams will play with team members missing and it can be a struggle to field a full squad. Of course the hardcore never struggle and are usually ultra fit from their season of indoor football.

When the summer comes , and boy is it hot, many serious teams enter tournaments either across the State, Region or even Country. The really serious teams will fly to California or Florida to compete in what is known as Select Tournaments. Some of which are by invitation only.

The kids I coached were playing every Sunday and practising twice a week. Most girls play for their town and some age groups can have up to three or four teams playing per age group. Everybody wants to play on the A team, and although the teams aren't labelled A and B, it doesn't really take a genius to work out which is which. Most teams are coached by what the Americans call a Pro Coach. This doesn't mean that you will see people like Bobby Robson or Sir Alex wandering around the local parks, it just means that the teams are trained by an Independent Football Trainer who is paid to run sessions. Many Pro coaches are British and I have to say that there is something about our accents and our history of football that brings with it an automatic respect. Most mums and dads are very athletic and have a history of playing basketball, American Football or baseball. The kids always made fun of my accent and at times did some fantastic impersonations -- but it was all harmless stuff. The Americans use different expressions to congratulate players so whilst I was yelling "Brilliant" or "Different class," everybody else was yelling "Good job!" or "Great boot!" I have since inherited the "good job" mode of encouragement and take some stick for this now I am back in the UK.

Girls' football in the United States is immense. They all start playing at around four or five years old. I would run programmes that were advertised as Soccer Peanuts or Soccer Scamps. You may well laugh, but basically this meant that a five year old would be learning a drag back turn, or as we called it a bubblegum turn, (you have to dress it up for a five year old) instead of learning it at eight or nine. So girls are immediately about three years ahead. At the age of seven they all turn out for the Under eight trials. The town will normally field as many teams as kids try out. So if forty girls come to the trials for the U8 girls team then the town will make sure that there are three teams for that age group. Teams are made up of around twelve or thirteen girls and they play eight aside on a small-sided pitch. The goals are slightly bigger than the mini soccer goals we use over here - which can lead to some high scoring games - which I hate to say - many Americans love. (something to do with high scoring games in basketball and American

football). The game at u8 is split into four quarters of twelve minutes. So after every twelve minutes the girls would come in for a drink and a team talk -- and of course the famous cheer such as "be aggressive, be aggressive be aggressive -- go sunbursts!" Need I say more? Much too outgoing for us reserved Brits!"

With most teams I would be left to pick the starting line up. Officially this was supposed to happen with every team (after all - this is why the parents pay for a pro coach), but occasionally you would encounter the protective father who just couldn't let go and had to see his daughter start every game and every game as up front, or as the Americans would say 'striker'. It's all about the goals after all. Sadly , like in this country, you would have ugly scenes of adults living their lives through their children and would yell and scream on the sidelines like their life depended on it. You don't have to be a child psychologist to see that kids absolutely hate this. I would send out newsletters to the parents of my players asking them to be quiet and not to yell any instruction whatsoever. Think about it --you could have spent three weeks practising playing the ball out from the back -- when a father yells "boot it out," and of course what does the kid do -- she boots it out like her dad is telling her to do, and then what happens, I stand on the sideline with steam coming out my nostrils and ears whilst everyone on the sideline yells " Great Boot." Absolute nightmare!

Most of the girls that I coached during my five-year stay were incredibly athletic. Many of them were playing at least two, sometimes three, other sports. Their fitness was pretty impressive and most of them could run and run and run. Role models who are advertising products on the television all the time surround the girls. They understand that to be the best in the U.S you have to be good otherwise you are just not going to cut it. At the age of eleven, girls are invited to attend try-outs for the ODP (Olympic Development Program). Basically this is a national programme that is run in every state. As girls get older more and more players are cut from the programme. This continues until eventually at U16 the organisers have pretty much decided who is worthy of a place for the National side for this age group. The Company owned an indoor facility, the kind that is popping up for youth team academies all over the place. It was a huge inflatable bubble, a dome with third generation rubber crumb turf. When I first set my eyes on it I could hardly believe it. A place where I could play and train all day, everyday - whatever the weather. It was like the mother ship calling me home ! Of course I carried my boots around with me everywhere and whenever I got the chance to go and kick a ball around I would be in the dome either smashing balls up against a huge kick back wall, shooting on anyone who would play with me, playing one on ones or practising long balls. I was fortunate to live close to a US National Team player for the U19 squad, Yael Averbush. We would play one on ones like there was no tomorrow, practice free kicks and shooting the ball. Often I was embarrassed at just how talented this girl was - but then I just had to forget that and get on with it. I was a defender who got to practice her tackles and Yael was a midfielder who got to practise her moves.

I guess practising with a National Team player made me realise just what it takes to make it to the top. If you think you practice enough I guarantee there is someone out there who is always practising twice as much and twice as hard as you are. Whenever I feel tired in sprints now I always think of Yael and know that she would never quit no matter how much pain she was in. Initially when I arrived in the States I signed up to play for a Sunday Women's League which was pretty relaxed. Although it was fun playing, girls just wanted to play for fun and wouldn't really take it seriously. I then found out one of the players was playing for a semi-pro team. I thought I would give it a try. I arranged trials with a couple of teams but when I spoke to the coach of the New Jersey Wildcats I knew that I would end up playing for them. The coach, Peter Wilson, was an Eastender, came from Bethnal Green, played for Leyton Orient in his hey day and was a leftie! As soon as I met him, we hit it off. I signed for the NJW in March 2000 and played with them for four seasons.

We played in the United Soccer Leagues W League. The League is divided up into regions and we competed with teams from the North East of America. We played teams called the New York Magic, the Boston Renegades, the Ottawa Fury, New Hampshire Phantoms and the New Jersey Stallions. We would fly to games and stay in hotels. We were given money to pay for lunches, taken to dinner, paid expenses and given really nice kit, tracksuits and bags. Staying in the hotels with all your friends was the best. Often we would have pizza parties after games and stay up talking about the games for ages.

Arriving at the airports was cool too. It was great turning up in our tracksuit and bags and strangers would look at us like we were famous or something. The games attracted quite large crowds and that took a little time to get used to. At some games the opposition would play music if you were taking a corner kick or if you had a shot on goal and missed -- weird but true. I absolutely loved playing. The intensity at practices was incredible. Everyone was playing for their place. I'm just so lucky that I'm left footed and unfortunately there are not many of us. I was happy also to play left back - so the competition for my position wasn't as tough as some players. The one thing I would say is that you had to be fit and relatively quick. The USL when I played in it was incredibly physical, fast, intense and full of female athletes who could run all day. I had the opportunity to compete with players who were sheer class. International players such as Meribel Dominguez, Kelly Smith, Rhian Wilkinson, Carly Lloyd, Yael Averbuch, Esmeralda Negron and Noelle Meeke to name but a few. Most of the teams were made up of Division One college players.

My team was a combination of Princeton, Penn State, U Penn and Charlston players. I probably played with two of the best centre backs in the female game and I have no doubt that if the pro league in America was still going they would have been approached to play. They are Leigh Hamilton and Heather Deerin. I learnt so

much from playing with such high calibre players and to this day I miss that win at all cost attitude and that feeling of coming off the training pitch feeling like I have done a few rounds with Lennox Lewis. I'm sure

many female players who are hitting thirty, look at the opportunities that are now available to young players and are so envious. I know I am. Female Academies are now being run in many professional clubs and the avenues to play abroad are more and more common place. I know that if I was given my chance to start again I would have studied in America and tried to play Division one football. Although I am envious, I am so happy that these opportunities are finally available for young girls. It's taken a long time to get to this stage and I hope the growth of the game and the developments continue.

# Pauline Cope Skills

## SKILL NUMBER TWO

1. Balance ball for a few seconds on foot.

2. Kick ball to knee-height

3. Kick ball up and flick leg over the top of the ball.

4. Catch ball with foot, kick up again.

3. Kick ball up and flick leg over the top of the ball.

4. Catch ball with foot, kick up again.

## SKILL NUMBER THREE

1. Balance ball on head for as long as possible

2. Lower ball onto mouth, balance for a few seconds.

3. Drop ball onto knee

4. Switch ball to other knee

5. Keep ball in air, and alternate knee-ups

6. Keep ball in air, and alternate knee ups

# It's a Child's Life

*f*ootball and children, children and football. It's a strange mix, some would say, an almost impossible equation, but two such players in the top flight of Premier League Women's football thrive on it. Mary Phillip, mother of two boys aged nine and seven, says organisation and back up help is the key to it all. When the boys were small and she coached other footballing kids at Millwall, the bottles and bags were ready alongside her trackies and boots, every day from seven am. A trip to the babysitter before work and off to the ground by nine. More bottles to prepare at lunchtime and then back to work for the afternoon. One particular memory is when her second son was born he had colic and screamed night and day. The babysitter wasn't available and she had to take him to training with her, the Manager at the time insisted he held the baby whilst Mary trained - and she could hear him screaming for a full forty five minutes -- the baby, not the Manager! Twice a week is training nights at Arsenal and this is where her parents step in, who she says, "Have always given me fantastic support, especially in the last nine years. My dad always thought football would just be a hobby of mine and that I could never make a career out of it, but now he's so proud and my parents always try to get to every game, including the England games, which involve a lot of travelling. My boys have not been that interested in football however. They'd rather play basketball, but last week my eldest came home from school and asked for football kit and boots! I rushed out and bought him some the next day, so maybe they'll become more interested as they get older. Meantime it's just something mum does each week. It's part of their lives and they are used to the routine. They probably think that all mums play football. They've never really known any different and of course it means they get to see their Grandparents a lot, which is nice."

*Mary Phillip*

*W*hen Katie Chapman joined Charlton last season, son Harvey came too. He is taken to matches and training sessions by Katie's partner Mark, who, she says, is a real 'hands - on' dad and can turns his hand to nappy changing and feeding whenever required. Like Mary though, Katie insists that it's not just about being organised, but the help she receives from both her family and Mark's, that enable her to have peace of mind when she is away with the England camps, often for days at a time. "With their help and knowing that he's in safe hands, means I can concentrate on my football and give it my best. Fortunately Harvey has always been a good baby and slept through the night at twelve weeks, so I can't blame lack of sleep if

I don't play well! He also plays football with his left foot, which is a bit uncanny, but I'm not surprised he's kicking a ball around at the age of two, because the girls at Charlton and the coaching staff all spoil him rotten and spend loads of time with him. He loves all the attention and it's like an extended family to him. Copey thinks the world of him and thanks to her he has a good bank balance too. Every time she swears, she has to put money in his piggy bank. So far he's doing really well!"

*Katie Chapman with her son Harvey*

# A Brief History of Women's Football in the Royal Navy

*t*he Royal Navy Football Association Women's structure is made up of individual clubs who are drawn from all RN & RM shore bases in the UK as well as all ships within the Fleet. Players from these units are selected to represent their associated Command of which there are three, comprising of Fleet (Ships and Submarines), Air Command, Scotland; Portsmouth; Plymouth, and the Royal Marines; from this the full Royal Navy representative team is selected.

Even though Women's football in the Royal Navy has only been active since 1997 and therefore is still under development, it has made considerable progress to date. There are only three thousand five hundred females serving in the Royal Navy with their ages ranging between sixteen to fifty three. From that only a small number approximately one seventy-five to two hundred or 5% would have played football of any sort. However; with the new influx of girls it is quite apparent that football is being better supported in the schools, thus reinforcing the Football Associations claim that football is the fastest growing female sport. In 1997 a 5-a -side competition was organised to gauge the desire of women within the Navy to play football, this competition attracted thirteen teams and it was those humble beginnings that women's football has grown.

## Cups and Competitions

Following on from the success of the first competition the first full eleven's competition was organised in which nine teams entered. The Navy now offers two eleven-aside and two small-sided competitions they are:

a. The Navy Cup, (open to all Royal Navy ships and establishments)

b. The Inter Command Cup (open to the three Command teams)

c. Indoor six- aside. (open to all Royal Navy ships and establishments)

d. Outdoor seven- aside. (open to all Royal Navy ships and establishments)

## Representative Team

The Royal Navy representative team play between ten and twelve matches a season with opposition being provided mainly from the South and South West of England. A selection of the teams we play are Cambridge University, Portsmouth Ladies, Yeovil Town Ladies, Plymouth Argyle Ladies, Sussex Regional Squad. The season culminates in an Inter Service competition against the Army and RAF, this competition started in 1999 initially between the Navy and Army with the RAF entering in 2001. Thus far we have been unsuccessful in winning the competition but have come close on occasions. The present representative team manager/coach has been involved with the team for three years; he is a B License Coach who is currently in his second year of his A License course. He is in the Royal Marines and finds that coaching the women's team is a welcome change to his everyday duties. He has stated that he enjoys the coaching women's football as they players are responsive and willing to learn.

## Future Development

Currently the Royal Navy has the following women coaches, one Level 3 coach, six Level 1 coaches and one Level 1 undertaking the Level 2 course. As more and more girls join the Royal Navy having been exposed to football we envisage that the quantity and quality of female players will increase. It is our intention not only to improve player development but also to increase the number of women coaches and administrators in order that they can have a greater input into the game.

# Susan Rea
# Soccer Player

Although the sport itself is the same, there are many differences between American soccer and English football. In America, 'football' is used only for that game with helmets and touchdowns, and 'shagging the balls' after shooting practice has an entirely different meaning! I learned to say 'boots', 'kit', 'pitch' and 'training' instead of 'cleats', 'uniform', 'field' and 'practice', and will now undoubtedly have to translate back again. As well as terminology, there are other variations on both sides.

One way in which I think that England outpaces America is in the extent of football coverage. Being in England for the 2002 men's World Cup and Euro 2004 tournaments was an amazing atmosphere and it was almost harder to avoid games on English TV than to find them, quite unlike back home! Although there currently is a professional soccer league in the U.S. for men, and was one for three years for women, the saturation of the sports market by baseball, basketball and American football has unfortunately left little media room for soccer. I also appreciated how easy it was to find a place to play in England. In the U.S. pickup basketball is common, but soccer mainly happens through organized teams or small committed groups. It was nice in England to have continual options for 5-a-side or just joining up on any grass area where there was a game in progress. Other differences that I noticed, however, offer room for improvement in England. For one, the commitment to conditioning and diet is much greater in the U.S. For my university team at Princeton we would train six days a week, at least three hours each session and with two sessions a day in preseason before classes started. And the only reason we didn't do more was because of legal restrictions from the National Collegiate Athletic Association. Even for my semi-pro teams over the summers, which only met together twice a week on top of games, everyone would do additional fitness on their own and keep an eye on food and drink more than I saw in England. Funding support was also higher in America, with several full-time coaches and physiotherapists, sponsored equipment and travel, and well maintained training and playing facilities considered standard even at youth club teams. Although the top level of women's competition in England may have similar benefits, the drop-off is very quick and opportunities for beginning players are much fewer. And even at the top level there are only a few teams available, requiring significant travel times (I would spend up to three hours each way on trains just to get to training sessions and home matches) for players.

In order for the women's game in England to develop, these concerns should be addressed. Furthermore, although the overall coverage of soccer may be less in the U.S., for the women's game the trend is actually reversed due to the Olympic and World Cup success and hence popularity of the Women's National Team, and among both boys and girls the sport is common at young ages. In England, however, I often found men surprised when they discovered that I played football, only really respecting that I could be any good when I played with or against them or when they watched our games for Charlton in person or on TV. Several of my teammates also had stories of not even having formal teams to play with when they were younger. However, there is room for optimism. Many of my male friends became true fans and were very supportive once they saw that women could play, and new clubs for girls are being founded each year.

I hope that the opportunities for girls in England to play football continue to grow, and that the recognition and support of women's football increase as well.

W hen I moved to England for my PhD study at Cambridge University, I was hoping to continue to play soccer as well, a sport in which I have participated through varying levels since I was six years old. I didn't know exactly what to expect in terms of the accessibility and level of play, but fortunately was happy to find many opportunities and experiences. In particular, I was able to play for two and a half seasons with Charlton Athletic in the Women's Premier Football League (still top of the table as I write this from back in California), competing in two FA Cup finals, winning the 2003-2004 League Cup and 2004 Charity Shield, and playing in stadiums such as Highbury, The Valley and Selhurst Park, and learning a great deal along the way.

Overall there were many lessons and ideas that I gained, but the main one was that sports create a bond across any divide. Simply by playing and training together, you learn a great deal about other people and have an immediate common ground to build on. In each team with which I was a part, whether Cambridge University, English Universities, Charlton Athletic, the engineering department or even just at weekly 5-a-side sessions, the passion for the game was remarkable. I will miss my football experiences, but the teammates, coaches, matches and training sessions that were such an important part of my time in England have left countless memories that I know I will always treasure.

# Sports therapy in
# Women's Football

*By Kate Rehill*

programmes may require me as the therapist to participate with the players to provide a role model for exercise, motivation, competitiveness, and for some fun. I also attend all matches whether home or away. Again preparation is mostly the same as before a training session. On match days my main job is to provide medical cover for any injuries that may occur during the game. If a player is injured at any point, it is my job to assess the injury and to make a judgement on the severity and whether or not that player can play on, and to administer treatment if necessary. In an emergency I would co-ordinate any back up if required, for example, an ambulance or a stretcher, as each case dictates. During a game I advise the reserves to warm-up every fifteen minutes to keep them on their toes. After a game, I assess and treat any injuries that a player may have acquired during the game, and also offer massage as a recovery aid. Along with the injury work there is a lot of administration to deal with such as, record keeping, exercise programmes, monitoring injury patterns, monitoring stock, and constant communication with players, parents, coaches, managers, and international medical teams. I also keep abreast of new research by up-dating treatments and putting prevention schemes into place. Working with Arsenal Ladies I have the opportunity to be involved closely with players on a regular basis. This has enabled me to be involved from the time of their injury to the return of a player to match fitness, and in some cases to watch them scoring the winning goal/s in the F.A cup 2004. Working with the team has also increased my appreciation of the importance of team dynamics, and has given me the opportunity to liaise with football coaching staff.

*a*s a sports therapists my role is to work along side the sports medicine doctor at Arsenal Ladies Football Club. I assess and recognise common orthopedic conditions and soft tissue injuries as well as being able to complete a progressive and effective rehabilitation programme for treatment and exercise for an injured player. My aim is to bring the player back to physical fitness in the shortest and most time-effective way. Working with a football team, I have found the need to be multi-skilled and to have knowledge of a number of areas such as nutrition, podiatry, massage, psychology, football, exercise and of course, sports injuries, to be invaluable. Essential on away trips, where people depend on you far more, you have to be understanding, open-minded, compassionate and flexible. I attend all training sessions with the team, before training begins. This is the time for preparing players, whether it's strapping, massage, or assisted stretching. Once training begins, assessments, treatments, and exercise rehabilitation programmes commence. Rehabilitation

## Injuries

Football has been reported to account for 50 - 60% of all sports injuries in Europe (5,7). This is a very large amount of injuries. This elevated rate has been attributed to the physical nature of football, as a contact sport. Collisions occur at any point of action or physical effort, increasing the likelihood of an injury. Physical contact only accounts for the smaller portion of these injuries -- about 44%, but the majority of the injuries 56% are from non-contact (1). Football places great physical demands on a player. In a game situation, a player will sprint every ninety seconds, lasting an average of two to three seconds, quick and short movements on and off the ball (8).

Twisting, turning, changing direction are a massive part of the sport. A player will turn around fifty times in one game, maintaining balance and control of a ball. Kicking and shooting both require a great deal of strength from the lower limbs, to create powerful and accurate passes It's also been noted that the demands are slightly different with different positions on the pitch (1,6,7,8). The incidence rate of injury in football is high. About 80% of female football players sustain an injury per season (4), and these are three or four times more likely to occur in a game situation, and will generally present itself in the second half of a game (6).

The lower extremities account for around 64 - 87% of the injuries in football (1,2,3,4,6,7,10). This is no surprise as the majority of football players use the lower limbs. Not so much for goalkeepers, who experience more head, face, neck and upper extremity injuries (6). Taking into account the physical requirements made on a player the knee and the ankle are responsible for 49% of the injuries and the most common type are sprains 66% of which are due to the forces that are placed on the ligaments (2).

Sprains in the knee are dominated by the Anterior Cruciate Ligament (ACL) sprain, which accounts or 47% of knee sprains in female football players (7). Female players are four times more likely to sustain an ACL than their male counterparts (1,4,9). It is still unclear as to the reasons why, but there are many ideas as to the contributing factors, which have yet to be proven.

The role of the ACL is to limit the amount of forward movement, and rotation in the knee, and maintains alignment of the thighbone to the shin bone. When a player twists, the ACL takes up 87% of the force required for turning, twisting, and changing direction, and if combined with contact, will increase the demands on the structures, hence the large amount of ACL injuries in football (9). The Medical Collateral Ligament (MCL) represents 28% of knee sprains, the MCL is to resist outward side motion of the knee, along with outward rotation of the shin bone on the thigh bone. More often than not a sprain occurs from non-contact, but major MCL injuries occur due to contact from another player tackling from the side and forcing an inward side motion on the knee. The other ligaments of the knee only account for a small percentage (8% )of knee sprain injuries (7). Another common injury related to twisting and turning is the Meniscus injury, and can occur in relation to ligament injury (9).

Muscle strains are the next common injury in football, Brynhildsen et al (1990) reported that in female football, the Adductors were the most frequently strained muscles 43%. In football the adductors can be overloaded when sideways kicking, pushing off to turn, changing direction, or in contact. There was very little difference between the Quadriceps 21% and the Hamstrings 20%. The

# Pauline Cope Skills

## SKILL NUMBER FOUR

1. Drop ball to foot

2.Bring ball back up to knee again

3. Bring ball up to head

4. Head ball up high and bend forwards to catch ball in-between shoulders. Ball rests.

## SKILL NUMBER FIVE

1. Start with kick-ups.

2. Kick ball up to knee-height

3. Flick leg over ball

4. Catch ball with leg and rest ball against bottom

Quadriceps are mostly caused by kicking a ball (86%) So, during kicking, they are in the process of shortening to produce a contraction. Therefore, when the foot comes into contact with a ball, it is adding resistance to the muscle contraction, and overloading the muscle (7, 8). The Hamstring has a great relation to sprinting, and this is thought to happen during running when the leg is coming through, and changing from a state of shortening to lengthening of the muscle (8). The most common overuse injuries in female football are shin split and Iliotibial Tract Tendinitis (ITT). Reasons for this are that due to alignment variations, women have wider hips, creating a bigger angle on the knees, and women's feet turn in more.

All these factors create a greater force on the shins and on the Iliotibial Tract. (2,6). Fractures are uncommon in female football and account for the least number of injuries in a season, but have a higher rate in adolescent's football. The majority of fractures 70% are a consequence of collision, and a small amount because of overuse (2). The growth in women's football may be accountable for the increase in football injuries, and the reasons for women being more susceptible to injury is yet to be proven and clarified. This is an area of women's sport that has to develop in order to work toward changing women's football for the better.

## Warm up

Football is a game of both physical and mental challenges. A football player's body is like a sports car. To reach the top speeds that the car can achieve and maintain, you need to gradually work through the gears to reach top speeds. So like a sports car, the football player should work through the gears to reach and maintain top performance. To perform to the best of their ability, a player should prepare, and, I don't mean by putting on their lucky socks, or making sure that they have shorts, shirt, and boots, I mean a warm-up. The warm-up has two main functions:

> 1. To enhance performance and exercise capacity.
> 2. For safety, and theoretically, for the prevention of injuries.

With these two reasons in mind, the next step is to look at how best a football player can activate both of these functions. A football specific warm-up, which is made up of two categories, is as follows:

> 1. General warm-up - Jogging, stretching, calisthenics, otherwise known as 'loosening up.'
> 2. Specific warm-up - Skill drills, small game situation, and a 'rehearsal' before the game.

When a football player is sitting down and resting, the body supplies 15-20% of its blood to the thigh muscles. When a player starts to run or kick a ball, a redistribution of blood occurs and an increase of 75 - 90% is witnessed in the working muscle, such as the thigh muscle. The increase in blood flow increases local vascular bed dilation, maximising muscle performance. Player-breathing rates will increase, and oxygen delivery to the working muscles is more efficient, reducing the production and the build up of Lactate Acid, and reducing fatigue. Due to the increase in activity in the muscles, the body will generate an increase in temperature, both to the core and to the muscles and at this point stretching should commence. The warming effect increases the elasticity of connective tissues and other muscle components, and aids in producing a smooth muscle contraction, which theoretically will reduce the risk of injury. Over the years it has been emphasised that static stretching is the way forward, but there are many conflicting

views on static stretching and its role in prevention of injuries. What is most agreed is that it enhances performance and reduces muscle soreness. Football requires quick and short change of direction, acceleration and deceleration. These demands on the body are dynamic movements, and therefore there is the requirement of more dynamic stretching in the warm-up.

1. Static Stretching - when a joint is moved by the person to the end of their ability (range), normal stretch to the point of tension and not pain.
2. Dynamic stretching - when the joint is moved as a result of a muscle contraction, demanding power and strength to stretch the muscles.

The coach, manager, physiotherapist or trainer, should always remember that unlike gymnasts, football players do not need hyper-flexibility nor to reach the end of their ranges. More specific movements such as ankle flick, wide skips, Russian walking and many more are more useful in preparing a player for football requirements. Warm - up is the time for players to mentally prepare themselves for a game. The warm-up is used to 'switch on,' creating mental alertness and concentration, by performing football drills, and mini games. Also, the time for an increase in a player's arousal level will occur and is needed for sports people to achieve optimal performance for a game. On match days the warm-up doesn't finish when the whistle is blown, the reserves still perform warm-up drills throughout the game. Peak performance is required from a reserve as soon as they cross that line, and may only have fifteen to twenty minutes left to play. The effect of a warm-up is documented to last around thirty to forty five minutes, but there should only be a ten minute delay after finishing a warm-up and enduring high intensity exercise.

## Recovery

A lot of money and time has gone into finding new ways of recovery after exercise, and ways to minimise any after-effects. There are a lot of drinks and supplements that claim that they are the best to help with recovery, but one of the cheapest and easiest ways to minimise the effect of exercise and reduce the risk of injury is a Cool Down. There are two functions for the cool down:

> 1 .To aid recovery and prevent soreness
> 2. To prevent injury.

A reduction in activity level of 50 - 70% of the player's maximum active level, is needed to return functions to a resting state. As mentioned earlier, the body redistributes blood when exercising. Via movement, the muscles help to return the blood back to vital organs. By reducing activity levels this allows for the washout and break down of by-products such as Lactate Acid. The removal of Lactate reduces the effect of Delayed Muscle Soreness (DMS), i.e. reducing the feeling of stiffness and soreness in legs the next day. A further reduction in activity by 25 - 50%, aids the body to return to circulatory resting levels, preventing blood pooling especially in the lower limbs, and preventing symptoms of light-headedness and dizziness know as Post Exercise Syncope. This is also a good time to stretch as the body temperature is higher than normal. Stretching will improve and or maintain joint range of movement, flexibility and reduce DMS. These stretches should be performed on the same muscle groups that have been used during playing. When performing these stretches, they are held for longer than in the warm-up. Thirty seconds each, aids in the decline of muscle tension causing it to relax. The duration of the cool down should depend on the individuals, and should last roughly between ten to fifteen minutes.

## References

1. Arnason A, Gudmundsson A, Dahl HA, Johannason E (1996). Soccer Injuries In Iceland. Scand J Med Sci Sports, 6, 40-45

2. Brynhilden J, Eskstrand J, Jeppsson A, & Tropp H, (1990). Previous Injuries And Persisting Symptoms In Female Soccer Players. International Journal Of Sports Medicine 11; 489-492

3. DeHaven K & Lintner D (1986). Athletic Injuries: Comparison By Age, Sport, And Gender. American Orthopaedic Society For Sports Medicine. 14(3), 218-224

4. Engstrom B, Johansson C, & Tornkvist H (1991). Soccer Injuries Among Elite Female Players. The American Journal Of Sports Medicine. 19(4), 372 - 375

5. Hawkins D & Fuller C (1999). A Prospective Epidemiological Study Of Injuries In Four English Professional Football Clubs. British Journal Of Sports Medicine. 33, 196-302

6. Inklaar H, (1994). Soccer Injuries; Incidence And Severity. Sports Medicine 18(1) 53-73.

7. Latella F, Serni G, Aglietti P, Zaccherotti, & De-Biase P (1992). The Epidemiology And Mechanics Of Soccer Injuries. Journal Sports Traumantol Rel. Research 14(2) 107-117

8. Peak Performance (Cited In) April 2004 Issue 196 Pg 11. Hamstring Strains The Most Common Injuries. Br J Sports Medicine. 2004; 38; 36-41

9. Peterson L & Renstrom P (2001). Sports Injuries 3rd Edition. Martin Dunitz, United Kingdom, Pg 273

10. Powell & Barber-Foss (2000). Sex -Related Injury Patterns Among Selected High School Sports. American Journal Of Sports Medicine. 28(3), 385-391

## Recommended Reading

1. *American College Of Exercise Testing And Prescription* 2nd Edition (1993). Williams & Wilkins, USA

2. Howley T & Franks B (1997. Health Fitness Instructor's Handbook 3rd Edition. Cheung K, Hume P, & Maxwell L (2003). Delayed Onset Muscle Soreness. Sports Medicine. 33(2), 145-164

3. Human Kinetics, USA

4. Mcardle W, Katch F, & Katch V (1996). *Exercise Physiology* 4th Edition. Wilkins & Wilkins, London

5. Pearson A (2001). *SAQ Soccer*. A& C Black, London

6. Witvrouw E, Mahieu N, Danneels L, Mcnair P (2004). Stretching And Injury Prevention: An Obscure Relationship. Sports Medicine 34(7) 443-9

# Points of View

## Wimbledon Captain
## Michelle Riley

Hunt

When Wimbledon men's team moved to Milton Keynes it looked like the end for Wimbledon Ladies, until the Dons Trust stepped in to rescue them at the last minute. Each player at Wimbledon pays annual subs of twenty five pounds, and the rest of the costs are met by the trust each year.

Riley

The players are aware that many other clubs have much higher subs and match fees, and are very happy with the set up at Wimbledon. As Michelle Riley says: "We have very loyal supporters and people behind the scenes who all want to see the club do well. Our obvious target is to gain promotion to the Premier League, and we are having a really great season. The fact that we do not have the financial worry of some players and clubs, means we can get on with producing good football. If we fall below second or third in the league this season, then we have not done ourselves or the club justice." Michelle plays centre half and wears the captain's armband. She is an old hand at Wimbledon having joined the club in 1992, from Croydon Ladies, who went on to become Charlton Athletic. Having been educated at a convent school she didn't start playing football until she was sixteen, so

quite a late-comer to the game. However, now twenty nine, and enjoying the game as much as ever, she is happy and confident in her role as captain. Michelle, a primary school sports teacher, starts her day at six am and fits in book-marking, parents evenings and school matches during her week. On three of these days she has training at Wimbledon after work and arrives home at midnight. It's a huge workload, and demands total commitment. "It also expects a lot from a partner if you are in a relationship, they have to be very understanding, but I simply love playing and the atmosphere at Wimbledon is strong. They are a good bunch of girls and

vary in shop and office work. It can be difficult for them to work their shifts around training and matches. In an ideal world if we could pay them wages we could all just focus on the football, but sadly I think that is a long way off. I also would like to see much more media coverage."

## Chairman of Coventry City Ladies
## David Singleton

*d*avid Singleton is in his third year as Chairman of Coventry City Ladies and has set up a structured organization to fusil the clubs ambition to gain promotion to the Premier league but to remain the friendly family run club as it is today. At the moment all players at all levels

we all get along well. The whole ethos of the club is family orientated so it is a happy place to play football, and when we win it makes all the hard work worthwhile."

## Liverpool Manager
## John Williams

"We are very well supported by the men's side now, which has made our lives much easier. We now travel to away matches in executive style coaches and all kit is supplied. Before their support came through we had to do all the usual stuff like arranging sponsored fun days and generally spending time trying to raise funds to keep going. Now it is easier to concentrate on the coaching side. We are having a good run in the Cup and I'm happy with the way things are going, but it is tough for the girls to attend training and work during the week. Some of our players work in the police and fire services, one is a manager of a hospital x ray department and others

have to pay subs each game, and this is one of the first things David wants to see erased. "All the players get involved with fund raising, by holding raffles and discos. This year some of them even did sponsored bag packing at our local supermarket! We are constantly networking, and first team player Julia Marshall is ever present on the phone to various companies. However with more backing we would stop subs immediately. One of our plans for the future is to develop a better relationship with the men's side. Coventry City Ladies have over two hundred and fifty players from eight years old to the senior side, and it is very well supported by the younger members' parents. We have some great players coming through our youth squads and Amanda Whalley, one of our home-grown players has just been called into the England U17's training camp. We are all very proud of her." Most importantly David, and Coventry City Ladies Manager Mark Phillips are of one mind when it comes to involving all ages in the game. At the end of the 2000/2003 season when they won promotion to the Northern league, the club organised an open-topped bus tour with the trophy, and were presented to the Lord Mayor. The tour ended at Coventry City men's ground where the girls were met to rapturous applause, and were introduced to the men's team. Some of the younger girls were mascots for the match against Stoke City, and as David says "It was a fantastic and memorable day, and all self funded! We are trying to create an environment where girls can prosper as an individual, and now I believe they can fulfill their potential to go right to the top with us."

## Chief Executive for Bristol Rovers Simon Arnold

Chief Executive Simon Arnold has supported Bristol Rover Ladies for six years and has seen a dramatic rise in the success of the team. When they played Arsenal in the FA Cup Semi Final two years ago, they attracted a crowd of over three thousand. A feat Simon puts down to solid advertising by the club. "We really pulled out all the stops. Posters, radio advertising, going into schools, ads in newspapers. You name it we advertised in it and the results paid off ! We are having a great run in the League and Cup this season but it is difficult to fund travelling and overnight stays. The men's team do help us out financially and we're grateful for that, but I would like to see more media advertising from the League, and make more clubs competitive in wages, otherwise all the best players will just go to the clubs who are co-joined to the big team names, and can afford to pay them. We cannot expect the same support from our parent club that Premiership teams are able to provide for their women's teams. The Chairmen of both Bristol clubs have been outstanding supporters of women's football in the region, and because both of them have taken the lead, the City of Bristol has had the opportunity to stage top flight football in the West Country this season. Whether they can justify this to their boards, shareholders and supporters remains to be seen. The league will become just a trickle of the clubs that are in it at the moment. Basically it all comes down to whose got the most money, which is a shame because the women's game is made up of people who play and support it because they love the game, and the commitment they have to the sport is phenomenal."

## Holland's Vice Captain Annemieke Griffioen

annemieke joined Bristol Rovers Ladies at the start of the season, to experience a different style of football and generally develop her career. Girls football in Holland has been slow to take off, but is now catching up very quickly, and Annemieke is keen to see her fellow country women take part in more friendlies and internationals. Without the participation, she says, "We will never be able to meet the standards of other European clubs. I think this will become better in the

future as more and more girls want to play. But for now, I want to concentrate on my game at Bristol Rovers and play the best I can for them. I am very happy here and the club has a great set up. I also work in an office and so I am improving my English all the time, which is good for me."

So how do the techniques vary from country to country?

According to Annemieke the game in England is tougher and far more physical. "But I would say the play is technically more advanced, and more skillful in Holland. However at Bristol Rovers there is more attention to detail, and the training can be quite strenuous. But that is because we want to be the best!"

## Watford First Team Manager Darren Ward

*i* have been involved with women's football now for four years and had hoped the game would have pushed on a bit more than it has. A number of reasons are to blame and these, I feel, are echoed throughout most clubs. I feel this is ultimately down to money and lack of direction within the FA rules. An elitism exists, and this makes the National Premier League boring -- lets face it, who'll win this year Arsenal or Charlton, Yawn! The real battle in this League is the one for survival. This same elitism is found in the Southern National Reserve League where our Watford team gets beaten by the top three clubs, Charlton, Arsenal and Fulham and then competes with the rest of the league to stay up. Arsenal reserves are a team that could quite possibly finish near the top of the Southern Premier League because they have that many good players. At Watford, like other teams, we do not have strength in depth to compete in two Leagues. While this is a goal we are aiming for, I believe there are two ways in which to make the Leagues more competitive now and to make women's football more exciting. My first wish would be for the football governing bodies to realise the problems that face clubs. They can help by implementing a 'Loan System' that would benefit teams like us. Good players I'm sure are playing in the reserve league and getting bored of winning so easily because there is no challenge for them! If they were put out on loan then the Southern and Northern Leagues would be more competitive, stronger, exciting and in turn so would the reserve league. Clubs and players alike would benefit. Secondly, I would like to see a transfer window like the men's game. We lost two players to the National League this year part way through, and with subsequent injuries, what we had hoped would be a challenge became a struggle. A transfer window then lets a player know that by signing, it is for a period of time and lets a club know her services will be available for that length of time. I think these changes would benefit the women's game and make it more exciting for all, I mean let's face it you all want to see Watford beat Arsenal one day, don't you?

# A Footballer's Life

**By Vanessa Raynbird**
**First Team Manager Portsmouth F.C. Ladies.**

i started playing football for a team at the age of fourteen which was thirty seven years ago (yes that does make me over fifty)! I played for a women's team, North Warnborough Ladies, as there were no junior girls teams in those days. I went on to play for Havant and Waterlooville, Southampton Women before ending my playing career in the National Division of the Premier League with Red Star Southampton (now known as Southampton Saints). When I first started playing it was with a group of women from the village who's husband, boyfriend or father had some association with the North Warnborough men's team. The attitude from the people involved was great. We had a male manager (father of one of the players) who respected all the girls. A few of the boyfriends and dads came to watch but nobody else. The attitude from immediate family and friends was fine as I started kicking a ball as soon as I could walk and grew up playing football with the boys in the street. In fact they used to make a point of calling for me to go over the field for a game. My parents were extremely supportive. My Dad was and still is extremely involved with the Basingstoke Football League and Hampshire Football Association and I think I was the son he never had and both my Mum and Dad always came to support. The attitude, from others however was not quite as favourable. Certainly the school didn't encourage it at all, it was always classed as a boy's sport with no opportunities at all, Luckily, I enjoyed a whole variety of sports anyway. The attitude of men who didn't have anyone they knew involved in the game was such that they didn't give it the time of day. Well there is now a structure in place for girls' football that runs from schools, to Development Centres to Centre of Excellences through to Academies. Similarly at club level, there is a good pyramid system catering for all levels of girls and women's football. So I think people have been encouraged to change their attitude towards girls and women's football. This has been proven by the fact that there are so many people, men and women, now involved in it. All that said however I think the attitude of the National media still treat it as a

subsidiary sport even though it is the fastest growing in the country! If you look at the back page of any newspaper how often do you see a women's face ! Attendances at games is growing in Cup Finals and at International fixtures but as a club that is lying second in the Premier League Southern Division we still find it difficult to attract any more than twenty or thirty spectators to our League games. Women's and girls' football is taken very seriously by all authorities within football now. The Football Association took over the running of Women's football in 1991, when the Premier League was formed, and we have never really looked back. In Hampshire we are extremely well supported and respected by the Hampshire Football Association who run very successful U18 and women's representative sides. There is a county cup which increases in participating teams each year, and I think we were up to twenty this year. They also have a lot of women on their staff especially in the Football Development and Coaching Department. Hampshire Schools also run an U16 representative side as well as having inter-school leagues and cup competitions. Non of this was available when I started playing football. There will still however always be the person in the street that will try and compare Women's Football to Men's and I'm not sure that you will ever get them to take it seriously. There is a structure in place from the F.A. regarding funding for Premier League Clubs (1st team and reserves) When travelling more than three hundred and twenty five miles we can claim for overnight accommodation to a maximum of one hundred and fifty pounds per match. We can also claim fifty pence per mile in excess of the first one hundred miles when travelling to away matches. There is also prize money available for the League Cup and F.A. Women's Cup. As a club we are very active when in comes to gaining sponsorship as it definitely plays a bit part in our financial position. We currently have a kit sponsorship from Perry's Peugeot Dealership in Portsmouth of two thousand pounds. We also have various sponsors that individual managers have negotiated during the season. This obviously only pays for kit and equipment and not the day-to-day running for example, pitches, referees, or training venues. We therefore have to raise money ourselves. We have a raffle at the end of each season, which normally raises three to four thousand pounds. We had a sponsored walk at Christmas along Southsea Sea Front, which raised two thousand three hundred pounds. Even with all this we still need to charge the players a pound per training session and a five pound match fee, as we have thirteen teams within the club. We do however encourage the players to get individual sponsorship to cover these costs which are approximately two hundred pounds per year, and certainly 80% of the first team secured this at the start of the season. Portsmouth F.C. donate one thousand pounds once in September and once in February. So we would find it quite difficult to survive without sponsorship but because of the passion and desire that we have at Portsmouth the players and officials would make sure that we survived without sponsorship by doing more fundraising. As a player with Southampton Women, I won the Women's F.A.Cup in 1981 and as a manager with Southampton Saints got to the Final where we were beaten 2-0 by Arsenal. Both of these achievements will stay with me forever. My main aim at Portsmouth is to keep developing the players to get them to such a level that we could compete in the National Division .

# Playing for Your Country

### Faye White
### Arsenal and England
### International

*f*aye White, England and Arsenal captain lives in Sussex and works in Hertfordshire. That's a two hour drive each way, every day, but she's not complaining. She realises she is one of the lucky few to be playing the game she loves, be part of a great team, and captain her country. For nine years, Faye played football and combined a full time job as a fitness instructor. She explains, "The company I worked for at the time were very understanding and were lenient with my schedule, but the more Arsenal progressed, the more time off I needed. I was also called up for England training camps and games including trips abroad. It was a terrible situation for both myself and the company". Then during a game, she ruptured a cruciate ligament in her knee and the serious injury meant almost a year out of the game - and work. Arsenal Ladies Football Club asked her to join them full time as part of their development team. The job entails visiting schools and encouraging youngsters into the game, which is very rewarding. She enjoys meeting the schoolchildren because, "the enthusiasm and energy these kids have is infectious and puts you in a good mood every day." So now, working for Arsenal also means she can have time off from the office to train, play football, and still get paid! But what would have happened if Arsenal L. F.C. had not stepped in with the job offer This is a major problem in women's football in England. "I am one of the very few lucky ones, speaking generally, most women have to decide whether they can have a career or play football. It is incredibly hard to combine both especially at the highest level. Players have to go to work all day, then travel sometimes as much as two hours to training grounds, train for two hours, travel back, and get up for work the next day, then travel to away matches on Sunday. Women do not play football for the money! They play because they enjoy the game, the team spirit, camaraderie, and of course winning and collecting silverware. Winning the FA Cup and the League with Arsenal have been the most amazing experiences and all of the hard work has paid off. Also at least once each season we play at Highbury after the mens game, last year we played Fulham in front of five thousand supporters, which was great." Faye, as ever, is looking to the future and is keen to keep the fitness door open, together with gaining her coaching badges. She would love to stay within the game when her playing days are over but is resourceful enough to know that coaching places are limited. She is keen to see women's football in the U.K. progress to the levels of other countries such as Germany

and the U.S.A., but says this can only happen when women's football stops playing second fiddle to the men's. "People immediately compare the men's and women's game, but they should not. It is a very different game. Also the structure of the game needs changing. It is very difficult to advertise a game, to encourage people along when the matches could be called off at the last minute. Pitches are not always available or up to standard because of the amount of play on them, and the men's games take priority. The attendances are not good at women's games - and this needs to be addressed. One of the ways, somehow, is to form a season that doesn't compete with the men's games. There is also too much diversity in club grounds and the facilities should be better all over, not just for the top clubs. Most clubs do not have full time staff working for them, and yet it is left to the clubs to cover their own marketing and advertising. Again this is hard if you have a full time job to do elsewhere. The media coverage has been poor in the past, but now that interest in the sport has taken off in the last three years, the coverage is getting better and the internet is a great outlet, together with Radio Five Live reporting on matches, and coverage by Sky Sports. Also there could be structural changes made in the game so that looking at the possibility of a semi-pro League rather than a professional League might be considered, underpinned with financial assistance and resources from the FA and potential sponsors, so that each club runs along the same guidelines, for example, playing contract, personnel, resources and the rest, providing a more stable base so that we don't get a situation where the movement of players can change the course of a club. Forming a fixture structure that is more rigid and easier for the spectators to follow, including forming an international fixture list so that all fixtures are the same for England, Scotland, Ireland and Wales. This also goes the same for Regional and County competitions. It would also help to make it a requirement for men's clubs to accommodate and support a ladies' team. This gives a firm statement that football really is for everyone, the whole community, ensuring that levels are improved then maintained and guaranteeing that better quality of understanding and knowledge is brought into the game at the highest level. We have taken massive strides during my fourteen years in the game, but it is imperative to keep looking for new ways to improve the game."

### Ciara Grant
### Arsenal and Irish
### International

" The Irish are very supportive of women's football and we get good crowds at Ireland's games, but when I was growing up in Ireland there were never any girls youth teams. I have been playing since about the age of ten just on the streets and then went straight into senior football at the age of thirteen. We never had an u10, u11, or u12 teams, and I don't think that has changed much now either. I think the game would improve more if they set up girls youth teams and brought girls football into all schools. I was lucky in a way that in my school we had a girls football team but not every school was like that. This would be a start anyway. It's hard because in Ireland the biggest sports are hurling, Camogie and Gaelic football so that's where a lot of the funding goes. It will only improve if more funding goes to women's football. Hopefully if the Irish senior team does well in the A Group, people will start to take us more seriously and put some money into it, which will open the door to other kids growing up. Things in Ireland are slowly getting better. We play on average eight games a year now, which is a big improvement. We have just won the B league so we will be in the A league next season and will play against teams such

as England Germany and the U.S.A., which will be great. But there is a large difference between footballing countries in how they look after their squad. For instance we do not get paid for games, only expenses. So we have to pay out first and then reclaim the money . But I'm not complaining, I'm really proud to pull on an Irish shirt. I would like to see more training sessions and more games though. I also agree with Faye that it would be much better to play directly after men's games for attendance, to show the supporters how good we are."

don't enter enough competitions? We need more teams being formed -- both adults and youngsters. I think it will happen in the future because the growth rate of girls playing the game is phenomenal and the resources will be found, I'm sure.We just need to market the game better, to get into schools and to let the youngsters know that there can be a future in football for them."

## Julie Fleeting
## Arsenal and Scottish
## International

*a*rsenal and Scottish International Scottish International Julie has notched up seventy three caps over the last nine seasons and is in her first season with Arsenal. She played for many school years as the only girl in the boy's team, until the age of thirteen when she joined an all-girls club. She has witnessed vast improvements in the game and is very optimistic regarding the development of women's football in Scotland. Girls in all schools now have access to the game

and regularly play other school teams at Secondary level and even in some primary schools too. Although the women still have to play on men's club pitches she says the structure of the game is good and is doing very well. "There is a great deal of encouragement from all areas of the game, and with football in schools for girls now, it can only mean a better future for all of those involved.

So many people are aware that girl's clubs exist now, which has meant the interest is growing all the time at a fantastic rate." Julie works as a primary school teacher in Scotland and so has her own programme for training and fitness during the week. She flies down to play with Arsenal at the weekends. It is a punishing regime, but one that she wouldn't change unless "the financial rewards from football could match a working wage. At the moment I have all my travelling expenses paid for, and things like kit and tracksuits are supplied, but it's a long way to go before I could give up the day job! However, the more we encourage sponsors into the game, the more I can foresee a time when women will be paid to play."

## Jayne Ludlow
## Arsenal and Welsh
## International

*j*ayne would love to play at The Millennium Stadium, in front of a big crowd, whilst wearing a Welsh shirt and her Captain's armband. But this in all probability will not happen because the Welsh do not enter competitions because they do not have the resources, and Jayne is very disappointed with the set-up. The Welsh lag far behind the other footballing U.K teams. She says, "There are lots of young girls wanting to play football in Wales, and I would love to be there to coach them when I quit playing. The interest is definitely there as it is growing all over the country, but how can you compete if you

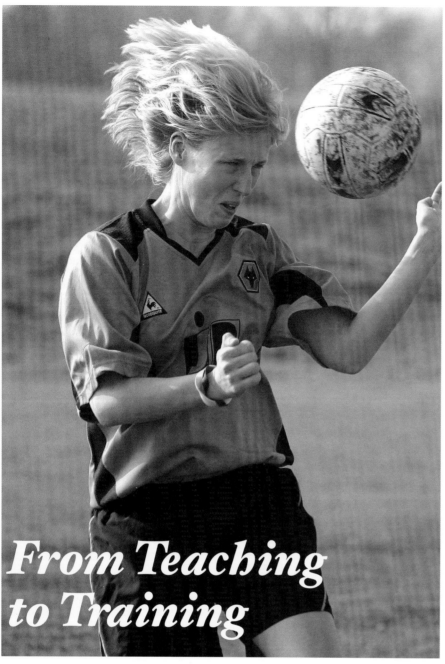

# From Teaching to Training

*Ann Blackham*
*Wolves Player/Manager*

**5**.50 am - Steve's alarm goes off, and off, and off every two minutes until he eventually gets up at 6am - it helps when I kick him out practicing for the opposition forwards!! He works in Manchester so has to leave at 6.30 am. I roll over and go back to sleep until he returns from the shower and puts light on. Thanks!! Curse the fact he works so far away and begrudgingly agree to make him some breakfast and lunch as he is running late. Again!

**6.15 am** - Make toast and sandwiches for both of us. Healthy diets obviously, and as I'm making the lunch, Steve has no choice!!

**6.25 am** - Shower and ready for work. Leave the house at 6.50. Journey to work usually takes about an hour as I live in Market Drayton in Shropshire and I work at The Coseley School Sports College which is near Wolverhampton. Chris Moyles is hilarious and I always listen to Radio 1 as it wakes me up in a morning. I text him once when in traffic and got a mention on Radio 1 - was a proud moment. He declined to play the Daniel O Donnell track I asked for. Boo. Always get slated at football for my love of Irish music.

**7.50 am** - Arrive at school and do a couple of admin jobs before some pupils arrive at 8am for girls' club. As we are a Sports College we try and encourage the pupils to participate in sport as much as possible, so we run breakfast clubs. Today is basketball but only five girls turn up so I am roped into playing a bit of 3 v 3. This leads to a rush up to staff briefing sweating and red faced at 8.45, as obviously I can't stop the game until our team are winning. First rule teaching PE - never let the kids beat you!!

**9.00 am** - One of the teachers in my pastoral team is away today so I have to do a register before going to teach period one. This starts at 9.15 and no one in my department is away today so I head straight to first lesson. As I am Head of PE it's up to me to sort out any work for supply teachers or cover staff. I hope I never again meet the grumpy git who once refused to take the kids outside for cross country in case he got the flu! On a sunny day, and we wonder why our kids are increasingly becoming fatter and unhealthier! Teach all morning -

Expressive Arts (classroom based ) with Year 7, racket skills with Year 8 and Circuit Training with Year 9. Eat my sandwiches at break whilst I check emails.

**12.25 pm** - It's dinner time and no time to relax as I round up the four Year 10 Junior sports leader kids who help me to run lunchtime activities in a local primary school. One of my roles at school is a School Sports Coordinator so I'm involved in raising standards in PE at our family of five schools. We go in my car, and again I have forgotten to clear out the mass of footie kit, boots and various litter from my car and they moan, as usual. Return to school at 1.15 and head straight for the water fountain when I realise my headache is probably due to the fact I haven't had a drink all day - not good preparation for training later.

**1.20 pm** - The bell rings and I return to the form group to do the pm register. Three kids are late which means I have to supervise them on late detention at 3.30pm. Great! Tuesday afternoons is double Year 10 which is GCSE group. I teach badminton period 4 and then monitor a member of my department teaching her GCSE PE lesson period five. Lesson goes well and give feedback whilst supervising late detention at 3.30. Have to be good at multi tasking when teaching here. Tuesday means primary schools football night. As part of the 3 Lions FA project we are developing opportunities for primary age boys and girls in football. Three schools are involved and approximately thirty kids. Ten of our Year 10 students help me to run the sessions as part of their work towards their Junior Football Organiser Award. Parents are there to watch so have to make sure the sessions are run well and kids are receiving quality coaching. This finishes at 5pm so all is quiet by about 5.15 pm when the equipment is all put away and the last child has been collected by parents. This is a chance to chill out for ten mins before I do some more admin work and plan lessons, and mark GCSE homework for tomorrow. We have training **from seven** to nine pm at Coseley. I managed to secure a reduced rate on our full sized astro turf pitch as money is a major issue at Wolves Women. Even though the board do loads of fundraising and we pay £5 a week subs, we have a very tight budget. Our school has a partnership with Wolves Women and the under 16s play here. I am currently writing a bid to the FA in order to receive funding to build a third generation pitch on site, which Wolves Women will play their first team games on. The school have been very supportive and given me time off curriculum to complete the paperwork, although it has been a difficult task and taken a lot of my free time too. The bid is ready to go except that in order to meet FA recommendations of a 65 % - 35 % split in terms of partnership funding, we still need to raise nearly £200, 000! We have approached Wolves FC but to no avail. It's difficult to raise money for women's football.

At 6.50, I go up to the astro to help manager Paul with the equipment for training. It's time to switch now from teacher mode to assistant player manager. Many of our players are similar age at fifteen or sixteen to the kids in my GCSE groups. Most of the time I help to lead the warm up and organisation but Paul and Dave, our coach, run the sessions as, having taught all day, I like to just get on with it. Paul and I discuss the session plans and I suggest we need to work on defensive corners for the important game against Sunderland at the weekend. We went to watch Sunderland against Villa last Sunday as our game was called off and noticed they were strong on set pieces. I find training difficult at times, sometimes it's hard to motivate myself as I am tired and have been at school since 7.50 am but most of the time it's enjoyable and a welcome release. It's difficult as assistant manager as I'm supposed to be an example and I have to admit I'm not overly keen on fitness training! After training will have a quick chat with Paul or sometimes go for a coke with some of the older girls. At twenty eight, I am the senior citizen by a good five years Mostly I get straight back though as it's a long drive back and I'm shattered.

**10ish pm** - and I'm back, and, if I'm lucky Steve has made the tea, good role reversal here! Mostly have chicken and pasta, he's not exactly Jamie Oliver. Then have a chat, watch tv for sports news and it's time for shower and bed.

It's now nearly **11pm** and that alarm is set for **5.50am**!!

# From Golfing Parent To
# Girls' Football Club Founder
## *How did that Happen?*

**By Tim Crook, Chairman and Founder of Assandun Vikings Girls F.C.**

### How it Started

*i*t was perhaps significant that at the start of a new century, my daughter, Anna, asked me to find a football team she could play for. My daughter? Play football? Surely, this was a male preserve! She was serious however, and I soon found out she was not the only one who wanted to participate in what was then the fastest growing sport in the country – girl's football – and this was before *Bend it Like Beckham.* The first problem was how to locate a girl's football team. Nowadays the girls' game is promoted more keenly by the Football Association and county FA's through schools, but even as recently as the year 2000, it was a very different story. I struck lucky. I happened to see a bright purple coloured advert for girl footballers in a local chip shop! After a few false turns, Anna

found herself a member of an under 11s team - one of two girls teams run by a large local boys club. Anna always had a natural ability and it seemed equally natural that her father should think he was bestowed with Sven Goran Erikson-like powers of coaching, and so I soon became coach and then team manager. I saw no obstacle in my lack of formal training and qualification to be a junior football coach. After all, Jose Mourinho was to win the European Champions League with Porto and he had previously been Sir Bobby Robson's translator! I now have a Level 1 FA Coaching Certificate and have learnt the error of my ways. It became clear very quickly that there were naturally talented girl footballers as there are boys and a lot of them -- all desperately needing teams, managers and coaches. The potential was huge, and to tap into that potential needed much organisation and support. As owner of the youngest team, I found myself looking after

60

an increasing number of younger girls as well as my under 12s. Those early years of being involved in junior sport were a new and informative period as I was unused to the ways and quirks of football club life. The explosion of girl's football, of which I was a part, and to which I was by now one hundred percent committed, led to difficulties in priorities for the club within which, the other girls team managers and myself were operating. Seeking support for our ideas and plans for the girls' section became a source of dispute, and I found myself looking at other ways to progress the girl's game in the local area.

## Creating a Girls' Football Club

*i*n the summer of 2002, I decided to explore the possibility of establishing a girl's football club, believing that the surge in girls wanting to play football was best served by a club dedicated to girl's football, and where the efforts and resources of all involved would be concentrated solely on the girls. First port of call was a phone call to the Essex County Girls Football league where its long-serving secretary, Tony Willoughby, gave me the low-down on what was needed. Tony's answer to my query about what I would need to do to start a girl's football club, went along the following lines:

*"You will need to create a club committee which must have, at*

*least, a chairman, secretary, and treasurer. Next you will need a qualified Child Protection Officer, and you will need a Club Constitution and Rules, plus,. you will have to register a Club name and an Affiliation number with the Football Association, here's a number for Essex F.A.."*

*"No problem,"* I said.

*"There's more"* he said, *F.A. and League registration fees will need to be paid, and you need to get Public Liability insurance. Here's the number of the insurance agent the League uses. Ooh, and of course, you will need a pitch.:*

*"Any more?"* I asked, trying not to let the panic show in my voice.

*"Yes* Tony said, (I somehow though he might). As *the players will be girls, facilities such as toilets are a mandatory requirement.. A privet understandably not being suitable."*
Tony left the best until last…

*"To register for this season, you will need all this to be in place by 15th of July."*

I checked the calendar -- four weeks to go! What had started as an interesting intellectual exercise was now suddenly Mount Everest!

But heck, I always wanted to be a mountaineer What happened next was a whirlwind of activity, as all I had was a bright idea and a great group of girls and parents who knew nothing about what I was up to. What were they to make of it all? I decided against telling anyone other than one or two people with whom I needed to share some of the issues to 'test the water', until I was sure the venture was possible, and then if I could not get the support necessary I would only have wasted my own time. I therefore concentrated on getting everything in place so that I could move quickly if I got support from the parents. I started with the last first as I figured that without a pitch nothing else was possible, and this was the hardest challenge. Finding available junior size football pitches for youngsters to play matches on was almost impossible, because schools will not hire pitches out as they do not want them ruined for the school team, which is not unreasonable really, and local councils had nothing available. It is no wonder that talent struggles to find its way through in the Nations sporting endeavours! Eventually I made contact with a Ewa McIlwaine, Sports Development Officer at Rochford District Council, who was an immediate enthusiastic supporter of what I was trying to do. She followed up a pitch-use

survey she had conducted and managed to persuade the outsourced, yes – they tend to be privatised, pitch administrators to mark out a junior-size pitch. I realised after some weeks of phone-calls and 'blind-alleys' that this would be the hardest challenge in the 'set-up phase' and I was jubilant when she told me the great news. During this period I had done the ground-work regarding registration, fees, insurance and constitution, having contacted the necessary people involved and obtained the necessary forms and other paperwork. The hardest aspect of this was choosing a Club name which had to be ready for the registrations. A new Football Association ruling prevented the re-use of a name, for example, a place name, which was already in use by another local club. This was a major restriction and called for much creativity as I wanted a name which meant something rather than 'Crook's Cloggers.' Angela, my wife, knew the history of the local area which was Viking-based, and the Viking name for where we lived was Assandun after a famous Viking battle. Hence the Club was christened Assundun Vikings Girls Football club. Everything was ready to go if given the green light. I now had the daunting task of presenting to parents with the opportunity that now existed and ask for their support that the initiative was going to need from them. I convened a team meeting with parents where I nervously outlined the issues which prevailed within the current club in terms of priorities and constraints, and the opportunity I had created for doing something new and exciting. I outlined that it was something I was committed to and would understand if they did not want to follow. A lengthy debate ensued where people were rightly concerned about a number of factors, mostly regarding the nature of current problems and the risks involved in creating and running a football club. The main area of concern was the financial input parent were going to be expected to make and the risks to the new club going forward. I presented a financial profile, as far as I was able to forecast, in terms of commitments and required funding, which helped paint a picture if not remove concerns entirely. To help in this regard, I had worked hard with Ewa to prepare an application for an Awards For All grant of five thousand pounds, which Ewa felt we were highly likely to receive, although this was not certain. It helped with the debate however as people were reassured there was money available from outside sources. Clearly there were going to be some risks involved and an enormous amount of effort required -- not least from committed individuals willing to comprise a committee. I could sense from the numbers of parents contributing and the nature of the questions and comments, that there was instinctive support for the idea and, as the meeting wore on, questions focused increasingly on how to make the idea work rather than how it was going to fail. The meeting took a vote and there was unanimous support for a new girls football club followed by a vote to adopt a club constitution, and a club committee was voted in. Looking back, I recall how nervous I was before and during the meeting but how marvellous the parents were. I had not wanted to compromise the positions of other managers in the club, and only broached the situation of the other girls' team managers immediately before the meeting. Dave and his team decided to follow us into the new club and Jim who managed the oldest girls team decided to stay. The paperwork was posted, the club was registered with the F.A. and the Essex County Girls Football League, the grant application was submitted and the teams established. Assandun Vikings Girls F.C.was off-and running!

## The First year

*t*he energy and enthusiasm people immediately gave to the club in the first year was immense and it is astounding to witness what a committed group of volunteers can achieve. We needed to raise money early, and within a few weeks we had held our first quiz night and raised three hundred pounds. We chased down annual registration fees from players and hunted sponsors down to fund kit purchase. A month later we had arranged, and held, a girls' football tournament attracting teams from all over Essex, which was a stunning success given the preparation time we had. We even made a little money which was a bonus. Then, in September 2002, financial stability landed on the doorstep with a five thousand pound cheque from Awards For All. This was a huge relief. The football season started with the club having two teams at u13 and u14 age-groups and both did very well. The club also worked with the Local Council in support of community sports events and a strong link with he Council was forged as the club became recognised as a community presence. The Committee pounded on and arranged a Christmas disco for the girls -- not to be repeated --and the club's first Presentation Night with all girls receiving a trophy of one sort

held in Southend-On-Sea. We have supported girls through the formal referees course and have five qualified girl referees. The club has put its managers through the FA Level 1 certificate training course and parents through emergency aid training.

The National Football Association Accreditation – Charter Standard Award, was achieved in November 2004 quickly followed by the Essex 'Club SX' equivalent. Expenditure in the first two years was enormous, as the committee sought to obtain the best for the girls. Our purchase of multi-size training goals has set the tone for other clubs who have noticeably followed suit since our teams started training with them. As money has got tighter, much work has been put into further grant applications and we successfully obtained a Local Area Network Grant of over seven thousand pounds. Club events have continued such as a club outing to the Women's FA Cup Final where we took over one hundred people, and we were able to attract a professional woman footballer from Charlton Athletic, Susan Rea, for our second presentation night in 2004. Susan also ran a coaching clinic for the girls and was superb throughout the weekend. The Club were also supportive in the creation of the new Essex County Girls Football League Committee when there was a question mark over its future in the summer of 2004. And so the work goes on. Assandun Vikings was created to provide opportunities to local girls wanting to play football and that is what it does, and the club takes pride in what it has achieved in such a short space of time. It has a positive presence in the households of many young people and in the community, and brings other benefits to the health and social well-being of the girls which cannot be understated. It is a force for good and this would not have been possible without all the support provided from many people in the early stages of its creation, and could not continue without the unstinting efforts of all the people who have been involved since then.

*Tim Crook*

or another. It was a great night, although nerve-racking once again. None of us had been responsible or actively involved in these kinds of events before so I marvel now at what we achieved in that first year.

## Growth and Development

*i*n the two and a half years since the early days, the club has more then doubled in size and currently boasts the most teams in the Essex County Girls League. Currently, five at different age groups, and we have over seventy girls involved with the club, which is growing all the time. We have supported Active Sport (Sport England) coaching programmes and run the Council's girls football entry to the Essex County Youth Games

# Referees' Anecdotes

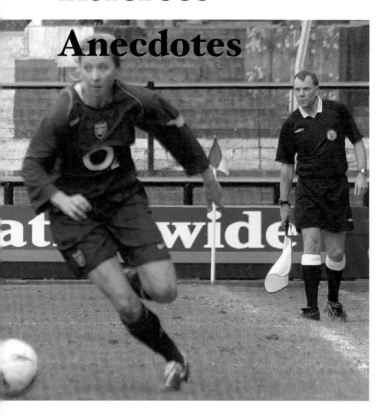

once refereeing a game and for forty five minutes the home team manager had been giving me absolute earache about every decision that I had been making. After the interval I came out and made my way to the home teams bench and duly sat down to await the arrival of the home team manager. On approaching me he said , "what do you think you are doing in the dug out?" to which I replied, "as you get such a good view from here I thought that I would referee from here, and stand a chance to make some correct decisions." This resulted in a number of his players starting to laugh and appreciating what had been achieved. During one match, I made a decision and awarded a goal kick, I then realized that I had made a mistake and changed it to a corner kick. A player soon pointed out the error but within a couple of minutes the same player made a mistake herself, and I had to point out her little error. We both had a bit of a laugh and smile and knew that it could happen to anyone. The one other thing is that the women themselves wish to be treated as equals when playing, I was at a game when the referee said to a player that if it had been on a men's game he would have cautioned her, to which she then turned round and said to the referee, what was the difference with the challenge that she had made and that a man would have made and if it warranted a caution then it should be given, she refused to back down until the caution was issued."

## Verity Waldney

"I am sixteen years old and I qualified as a referee last June. I had been playing football for six years and I felt I wanted to become even more involved with the game. Two of the main reasons why I chose to do this were first to encourage girls to follow my example and also to earn some money whilst doing something I enjoy. The first time I refereed I was very nervous and had to double-check all my kit and equipment. The main disadvantage of the job is the abuse from some of the supporters shouting from the sidelines. You learn to block out the shouting and just get on with the job, as after all, the referee's decision is final. I would certainly recommend more girls to consider joining me."

## Paul Barett

"This is just a quick insight to the role of referee at the Women's game at all levels Having refereed Men's adult football for a number of years, I was asked if I had ever thought of refereeing Women's and girls' football, to which I had not at all given a glance, so in 1999 I asked to go onto the South East Counties Women's Football League. My first experience of the game was to say the least uninspiring and I wondered if I had made the right decision. I was in Buxted on a very wet Sunday afternoon with changing facilities that were not the best and where the power kept failing! But as the season progressed things started to get better and the games and competition improved.. At the same time I was also asked to act as Assistant Referee on the Women's Premier League, and found the standard to be altogether of a different level. At the end of that season I was rewarded with the SECWFL League Cup Final which was held at Woking F.C. and so the mould had been set. I was invited onto the Referees List of the Women's Premier League for the season 2003/04. One of the hardest things to accept was the fact that a lot of my male colleagues found it very hard to believe that you can get enjoyment out of women's football. They also believed that the skill level is nowhere was good as men's. This attitude still exists today, but by inviting them along to games one or two heads are beginning to turn. Looking on the brighter side I was

of the day it's your decision. You took the course, you know what you're talking about, and only you have the control to send away from the touchlines, anyone who is shouting abuse. I'm a lot more confident now and thoroughly enjoy each experience, but I have to admit it was a fairly tumultuous start to my refereeing career."

## Jennifer Lidbury

"I was booked in for a weekend referee course which was run by The Essex County FA at Essex Police Training Centre in Chelmsford on the 26-27/6/2004. The course took place over the Saturday and Sunday 9am to 5pm. When I arrived on Saturday morning there were about thirty people, six of them were girls (including me) aged fourteen and upwards. The first thing that happened was everyone was given an eye test, and then we were split-up into three groups. Then were all given some books, which contained all the laws covering the game that a referee must know. Over the course of the two days I was taken through these laws both inside the classroom and outside on the football pitch to make sure I understood them. At the end of the two days I was given an oral and written exam. To become a qualified referee I needed an

## Charlie Twydell

"Refereeing is all to do with confidence. Everyone dreads their first match. Refereeing on their own, knowing that every decision they make will reflect on the outcome of the game. This can be a really exciting time for some people. Usually their first match will be fine and they'll find out that there's really nothing to worry about. However my first match will be one to remember. I had to deal with situations on and off the pitch and the decisions I made would definitely make an outcome.  It started off just like any other Sunday League game match between two evenly matched girl teams. The game was going really well and I felt that I had succeeded. Until it came to the end of the first half where I missed a couple of offsides and things began to build up on the side of the pitch. The linesman began to shout at me.  At this point he didn't know it was my first game. Then the parents from the home side got involved and then it all kicked off! There was a lot of shouting and swearing from one of the adults. I was very nervous when it came to half time, but I stood my ground like any ref would and I walked over calmly, took a deep breath and sorted it all out. But it was very  unpleasant, although a good learning curve. The fact of the matter was it was my first game. Everyone misses stuff, it's not like I was deliberately doing it to make the score line biased. With every mistake you make it makes you a lot stronger the next time. The key point of this was that I didn't get scared of the man, or what was happening and kept my cool at all times. I got them to spilt up and the supporters had to stay on different sides of the pitch. The advice that I would give is when refereeing matches, remember that you are the person in charge and at the end

overall  score of at least 75%. Everyone on the course that weekend passed. My tutors were really helpful and kept going over topics making sure that I had remembered them. Despite being qualified, the thought of refereeing for the first time was frightening. As I was fourteen years old I could only referee children who were twelve and under. My first few games were at a boy's 5-a-side  tournament under the guidance of a seasoned referee, this was very helpful and helped to boost my confidence."

# UEFA European Women's Championship

*t*he two-week event from Sunday 5th June to the Final on Sunday 19th June 2005 is the perfect opportunity for the England squad to show their elite players to the World. Stars like Captain Faye White, very vocal, always encouraging the players, leading by example, striker Kelly Smith, now back from playing in the USA, and recovered from a broken leg, together with midfielder Katie Chapman, will give the young England side the experience and leadership required.

The tournament, to be staged in the North of England, home to the most hardened of football fans, is expected to see crowds of around twenty five thousand. "We hope to attract the biggest ever live audience to watch women's football. This will enable the FA to tell young girls all over the country about the opportunities now open to them to play football. We expect participation levels to rise again sharply after the tournament, and the England players will become role models for future generations," says the FA's Director of Football Development Trevor Brooking. The tournament will be shown live on Eurosport and on terrestrial television. It should mean perfect timing for the England players to grab televised foot

ball coverage, but physically it will be tiring as they are playing back to back from the League and Cup Finals.

However, captain Faye White is sure the players will respond to such a big showcase opportunity. "It is the best tournament to have happened in England in years, we are training well and have belief in ourselves. We want to show everybody just what we are made of. We are a skillful team with just the right mix of experience and new girls coming through on the international stage, and I really believe we will do well this year. I think we played very well against the Italians in February and we had a good Algarve Cup run, and this has inspired the whole team."

The last time England competed in the UEFA Women's European Championships was in 2001,when they faced the two toughest teams in the Championships, Sweden, and this year's favourites Germany. England qualify automatically as hosts this year and the draw, which took place on the 19th January, has England in Group A alongside Finland, Denmark and Sweden. Group B features Germany, France, Norway and Italy. England has yet to lose to the Finns, so Coach Hope Powell is very happy with the draw. "The opening game suits us and we are all looking forward to playing at Manchester, in front of a big crowd, we know we have a tough task ahead but strong support from the fans will help us." England has also played well against the Danes in previous meetings and has five wins to their credit. However they have only beaten Sweden once in fifteen matches and the Swedes are the favourites to win Group A.

"They will be difficult opponents, but they are not unbeatable, says Hope Powell, we will certainly be looking for a good result from that game as well. The most important thing now is our own preparation, and that is looking great. The girls are very buoyant, especially after the win against Italy and our display at the Algarve Cup. We are totally committed to doing well in this tournament."

If the way the team played in the Algarve Cup is anything to go by, we are all in for a treat. The English girls showed they could compete with the best and put on tremendous performances, even though they were without some of their more experienced players, due to injury. Losing out to China on penalties was tough, but nevertheless learning curve for the younger girls in the team, and good preparation for the Euros. June 5th is just around the corner for these girls to show how much women's football has progressed over the last few years. If England prepare well, play well and get some good results, we can all enjoy an entertaining European Championships, and then look further ahead to a cracking 2007 World Cup in China.

# List of Schools of Excellence

Arsenal
Aston Villa
Barnsley
Birmingham City
Blackburn Rovers
Brighton & Hove Albion
Bristol City
Cambridge United
Charlton Athletic
Chelsea
Colchester United
Chesterfield
Coventry City
Doncaster Rovers Belles
Everton
Fulham
Gillingham
Ipswich Town
Kidderminster Harriers
Leeds United

Leicester City
Leyton City
Lincoln City
Middlesbrough
Millwall
Northampton Town
Norwich City
Notts County
Plymouth Argyle
Reading
Sheffield United
Shrewsbury Town
Southampton
Stockport County
Stoke City
Sunderland
Tranmere Rovers
Watford
Wimbledon
Wolverhampton Wanderers

# The Colchester United
## Centre of Excellence

*f*ollowing the ongoing development of the Female Development Programme at The Colchester United Community Sports Trust (CUCST), plans were formulated and implemented to allow previous hopes of establishing a Female Academy to become a reality. Forging a working partnership with The Thurstable Sports College, and submitting an application to The Football Foundation to finance the project were key components in realising this dream. The Academy programme aims to enhance provision and opportunity for female footballers by offering post-sixteen education courses and a structured football, team-based coaching programme. Providing exit routes beyond the current Excellence Programme and increasing the standard of the women's game locally, regionally and nationally are key targets, in addition to ensuring students can access higher education beyond the completion of the Academy programme. The programme will also provide sports-coaching and leadership courses, specific football coaching courses and practical football coaching experience to support the main programme thrusts and to provide all students with a broad education encapsulating many career and further education pathways.

## The Need

Over the last three years, Colchester United Female Centre of Excellence has seen twelve players graduate from its programme and move into other football schools or Licensed Academy Schemes. Whilst during this time, CUCST has been working towards achieving Academy status, it has been very frustrating to see players who have developed over a sustained period of time take their abilities to other clubs and programmes. This has further motivated our staff to work towards establishing a Colchester United Female Academy with key partners, ensuring that a scheme is operational, nationally recognised and licensed by the football authorities. This will allow CUCST to achieve its ambitions in providing a structured pathway for girls beyond our excellence programme and increase the standard of the women's game, fulfilling the aspirations of many talented female players, particularly those who have committed themselves to Colchester United historically.

## The Programme

CUCST primarily prioritises the education of Academy students and will allow the football programme to evolve from the framework of the education timetable. A minimum of eight hours per week will be football-focused, which will include blocks of time devoted to the following activities, and these eight hours will be split into three or four blocks of time during the course of the student's week:

1. Football coaching programme - Delivered by a coach possessing the minimum of an FA (UEFA B) Coaching License and directed by an FA (UEFA A) Advanced Coaching License holder, the programme will be structured to improve all aspects of the student's playing game with particular focus upon the development of game understanding and tactical awareness to further add to the previous player development pre-sixteen. This will take place at The Thurstable Sports College, making use of their third generation turf pitch and excellent grass pitch provision.

2. Fixture programme - Registered within the British Colleges Sports programme the Colchester United Female Academy will fulfill a comprehensive fixture programme against a variety of different opponents. Incorporating games against other FA Academies, competing in National College competitions and fielding sides against other schools and colleges from the Eastern region, the Academy students will experience a range of competitive opportunities.

3. FA Football Coaching Awards/ Sports Leadership qualifications. In the first year all students will complete the FA Club Coach Level 1 award and the Community Sports Leader Award (or equivalent). The second year will see all students complete the Higher Sports Leader Award (or equivalent), a second sport coaching qualification (e.g. Hockey Leaders, Basketball Leaders etc.) in addition to suitably motivated students being encouraged to undertake the programme of learning required in achieving the FA (Level 2) Coaching Certificate.

4. Practical Coaching Experience - To complement the above awards, students will be involved in the delivery of football coaching activities at both The Thurstable Sports College and as part of the programme of activities delivered by CUCST. This will add practical experience to aid the completion of the qualifications mentioned and enhance the development of students' interpersonal skills. Week to week the constitution of the students' football activities will alter. The frequency of fixtures, specific preparation for games, the content of the coaching programme, duration of coach education courses and educational commitments will define each weeks programme, although the target is to deliver a minimum of eight hours per week. The programme of activities will be timetabled annually ensuring that a necessary structure is implemented.

# Pastoral Support

## Education

The Thurstable Sports College will be responsible for ascribing students with individual tutors to ensure the necessary support and guidance is offered with regards to their experience at the college.

## Football Programme

An Academy Manager will be appointed with full-time responsibility for managing all aspects of the football programme including supporting the students with any issues that may arise through their involvement within the Academy.

## Home Stay

Suitable lodging facilities will be sought for all players expressing a need for such a service. Students, where appropriate, will be housed with local families who will undergo a series of rigorous testing procedures to ensure their suitability for providing a welcome, homely, safe environment for young females aged sixteen to nineteen. Financial support is available and can be located through the Further Education Residential Support Scheme (FERSS) or the Education Maintenance Allowance (EMA). CUCST can provide information assisting in the location of such funding but it is the responsibility of parents to apply and secure any means-tested monies required. CUCST understands its responsibility in terms of ensuring the provision of a safe home for Academy students, and will provide weekly support to all students who choose this option.

# Exit Routes

## Higher Education

Through the completion of their education courses, students can seek pathways into higher education. CUCST will during year one of the Academy programme, identify suitable, specific gateways for its students. The extensive, broad programme of activities will ensure that the students are well equipped for higher education. The combination of sporting excellence, academic achievement and practical sports coaching and development experience will ensure that students have a well-rounded portfolio to present to Higher Education institutions. Avenues into scholarships to American Colleges will also be investigated and opportunities for application by suitable students encouraged. A student's educational achievement will determine how realistic a goal the higher education pathway is.

## Sport Specific Employment

The successful completion of sports coaching and leadership awards, both football-specific and more sport generic, will provide students with the qualifications and the practical coaching experience to support applications to organisations specialising in the delivery and/or development of sporting activities. CUCST itself operates an extensive sport and social development activity programme, where employment opportunities arise for interested, suitably qualified people in addition to it being one of the best recognised sporting charities in the country, with a vast range of partners and supporters operating in similar, yet wide-ranging fields.

## Playing Opportunities

As part of the National FA Licensed Academy Programme, girls may graduate from the scheme into International squads and/or National League sides. Colchester United Ladies F.C (currently Southern Combination members) will also provide playing opportunities for all Academy students.

It is also expected that all students will participate within exit trials at the completion of the Academy programme, attended by scouts and representatives from a variety of clubs and educational institutions to allow the students to sell their playing abilities to interested parties.

## Targets

Number of Players

| | |
|---|---|
| Year 1 | 10 |
| Year 2 | 10 |
| Year 3 | 8 |
| Year 4 | 12 |
| Year 5 | 10 |

The emphasis of the programme is quality over quantity. The targets established below are a realistic yet demanding goal. To have 80% of students within higher education or sports-specific employment beyond the two-year programme confirms CUCST's commitment to individual student development as people as well as players.

| | |
|---|---|
| Progression to University Scholarships* | 20% |
| Progression to University (UK)* | 40% |
| Progression into Sports Coaching/ Development Employment* | 20% |
| Progression into International squads | 4% |
| Progression into National League sides+ | 40% |
| Successfully Completing Educational Courses | 90% |

\* Within 12 months of completing the Academy programme
+ Within 24 months of completing the Academy programme

## In Summary

Whilst the programme is new, it is ground-breaking in Essex, and in terms of Football Association licensing, in the Eastern region. CUCST's provision of such a scheme is untried, yet our experience in developing girls' football is established amongst the foundations of the overall progression of the game nationally. Within the first twenty clubs to attain a Football Association license to operate a Female Centre of Excellence, the first nine nationally to enter into a recognised competitive framework, competing on equal ground with the top clubs in Europe, Colchester United is now keen to further its reputation in providing excellent football playing opportunities beyond the Centre of Excellence programme. Through the partnerships developed with The Thurstable Sports College, The Football Foundation, Essex County Football Association and The Football Association on a national level, CUCST is excited by the

prospect of the Academy programme being recognised amongst the best in the Country. The players progressing successfully through the programme will hold excellent credentials to further their careers along whichever avenue they decide and to continue to establish Colchester United among the top female football developers in England.

# The National Premier League

-  **Arsenal LFC**
- **Birmingham City LFC**
- **Bristol City WFC**
- **Bristol Rovers WFC**
- **Charlton Athletic LFC**
- **Doncaster Rover Belles FC**
- **Everton LFC**
- **Fulham LFC**
- **Leeds United LFC**
- **Liverpool LFC**

# History

*A*rsenal Ladies FC was formed in 1987 by the women's present General Manager and men's present kit manager Vic Akers. In its seventeen year history, nineteen major trophies have been won, including two domestic Trebles, six Premier League Titles, seven National League Cups and six FA Cups, proving that the Ladies team really are the present dominant force in their domestic game. Arsenal Ladies FC have excellent backing and support from Arsenal Football Club. Mr David Dein, is the men's vice chairman and is the club's President, and Clare Wheatley, assisted by Ciara Grant and Faye White, are employed by Arsenal FC solely to develop and coordinate the female side of the club. A further three senior players also work at the Academy overseeing the youth development of the

*Captain Faye White lifts yet another trophy for Arsenal*

club. The club has continued to development as the Ladies turned semi-professional in 2002, allowing the players to continue to set the standards at the top level of the game as they receive financial recognition as footballers at Arsenal FC. The 2003/04 season proved to be a fantastic season for the ladies, where they more then made up for the lack of silverware the previous year. Finishing the season as double winners, they clinched the FA Cup with a 3-0 victory over Charlton in front of over twelve thousand fans at QPR FC, and live on BBC 1 with an audience of 2.2 million. They then confirmed their qualification back into the UEFA Cup, after sealing the League title with a 3-1 defeat of Fulham Ladies at Highbury in the last match of the season, in what was the most competitive league title challenge. This season will see the ladies represent England for a third time in four years, where they will at least try to match their best efforts as semi-finalist in 2003. The club as a whole proved that there is phenomenal talent for the future with the reserve side also collecting their respective 'Double'. Winning the reserve league in style, fin-

ishing the season unbeaten as well as collecting their fourth consecutive League cup title in as many years, the u16s also finished their season unbeaten in the Centre of Excellence league that covers the whole of South East England. An achievement that now sees them complete two years in a row without dropping a single point, proving that there is phenomenal talent for the future with competition for places, meaning a very bright prospects for the 2004/05 campaign. Over previous years, Arsenal Ladies have also claimed the fantastic achievement of a tremendous domestic treble in 2000/01, and then following that by being crowned champions again in 2001/02, making it to date a total of six times as League Champions since 1992. The 2002/03 season again saw Arsenal Ladies have a very successful year, however by their own standards, the lack of a trophy left the players and management frustrated and disappointed. The ladies finished third in the league by a point, reached the League Cup final and lost only on penalties, made it to the FA Cup semi-final as well as proving them-

selves to be one of the top four teams in Europe. They also progressed through to the UEFA Cup semi-final only losing to a very strong Danish team. After a successful group stage, which they hosted, and saw them finishing top. Previous to that in 2001/02 their first experience in the Women's UEFA cup saw them reach the quarter finals, losing to Toulouse. Over

*Fred Donnelly*

ARSENAL LFC

16, 14, 12, and under 10 levels in the NIKE Centre of Excellence, and are planning to expand further with an under 8 team. Arsenal Ladies have continued to play their part in the development of the game. Their established Soccer Schools provides the opportunity for girls of all standards to be involved in the game. Whether it be introducing girls to the game for the first time, or providing some competition for those who have been playing longer. The soccer schools are designed to offer girls aged seven to fourteen the chance to see what football has to offer and continue to bring opportunities to more and more potential players in a fun and relaxed environment. The Ladies teams have representation at International level wherever possible but in addition, have forged closer links to countries around the world. The club still continues to receive enquires from internationals from Portugal, Brazil, Nigeria, Japan, USA, Australia and New Zealand. Presently the senior ladies team boasts more than fourteen internationals.

*General Manager Vic Akers discusses tactics with Jayne Ludlow*

the years as well as playing in Europe the ladies travels have taken them literally all around the world, starting with a trip to the USA during the summer of 2002 to play the USA National Champions, San Jose Cyber-Rays. With a crowd of over five thousand, the England representatives narrowly lost 2-1 to a team who were mid season and professional and included some of the best international players from around the world. The ladies were invited to Nigeria to play in a match against the Nigerian National side for the Kanu Heart Foundation. The reserve team is mainly made up from the girls in the Arsenal Youth Academy, which continues to prosper. The Academy is run under the guidance of Fred Donnelly. First team players Jayne Ludlow and Emma Byrne also joined the Academy as full time staff. The Arsenal Ladies Academy enables players aged between sixteen and nineteen to combine daily football coaching with academic study. In 2002/03 Arsenal Academy provided a third of the players in the England Under-19 training squad. Arsenal Ladies also run teams at under

## Arsenal LFC Who's Who

**President -** David Dein

**Manager -** Vic Akers

**Assistant Coach -** Fred Donnelly

**Sports Therapist -** Kate Rehill

# History

**BIRMINGHAM CITY LFC**

### In The Beginning

**b**irmingham City Ladies FC was formed in 1968 by a group of girl supporters, and friendly games were played locally up until 1970. The late John Lines played an influential part in those early days and the club thanks him and all the players. In 1970 the Heart of England League was formed. The Blues remained in this league until 1973, and due to the restructuring of the leagues, later

became members of the West Midland Regional League formed in 1974. During this period Birmingham City Ladies won numerous League titles and cups notably in the Seventies and Eighties. To this date the Blues remain the only West Midlands team to have reached the WFA Cup semi finals. (73/74, 87/88 and 03/04 seasons.)

### A New Era

In the late nineties Birmingham City Ladies enjoyed an influx of new management personnel. Marcus Bignot and Michael Moore took charge of the playing side of the club and Steve Shipway, took over as Chairman, and reshaped the commercial affairs of the club. These 'new faces' added to

the vast experience already at the club in secretary Sue Hector and fixtures secretary Fiona O'Driscoll. These changes stood the club in good stead for development. In 1998, the Blues won promotion to the newly formed Combination League and at their first attempt won the League and gained automatic promotion into the National Northern Division. The club continued this fantastic run by winning promotion to the National Premier Division after only two seasons. The 2001/2 season saw BCLFC as champions of the Northern Premier Division and League Cup finalists. These on-field achievements, coupled with acquisition of Charter Standard and a heightening of public awareness of the club, led to the award of FA Club of the Year, and a highly successful season was completed. Two seasons spent establishing Premier Division status convinced the club that the next step forward had to be the transition to semi-professional status. The departure of Eniola Aluko to Charlton Athletic in January 2004 merely endorsed this decision. The club became a limited company in September 2004 to enable more lucrative sponsorship deals to be brokered. Unlike most of the top women's clubs, Birmingham City Ladies receives no financial or logistical support from the Men's Club, making the commercial activities absolutely crucial to the clubs growth.

### Grass Roots

In recent years the youth policy has proved invaluable and all the hard work is now coming to fruition. Birmingham City Ladies currently have more players representing England in the full squad than any other club, as well as players in the

u21, u19 and u17 squads. The club runs a successful junior section catering for girls from eight to sixteen years of age who play in the Central Warwick League. Granted a School of Excellence in 2001, and starting an Academy in conjunction with Solihull College a year later ensures the development of the younger players to future stardom. The club holds Charter Standard Community status and also Charter Standard Adult status, winning Adult Charter Standard Club of the Year in 2002/3 to complement the recognition as FA Club of the Year in 2002.

## The Future

Having taken the step to become Semi Professional at the start of the 2004/5 season, the club now moves into the top echelons of women's football, and the challenge is to stay there. Receiving no financial support from the men's club, makes the task of competing with the clubs around them even more daunting. Commercial activities are ongoing and the immediate aim is to win major trophies in 2005/6 to build on this season's achievements.

Every club is built around the people behind the scenes and BCLFC are fortunate to have the completely voluntary services of many hard working and experienced personnel.

*Amanda Barr celebrates*

**Birmingham City LFC
Who's Who**

**Chairman -** Steve Shipway
**Coaching Staff:**
Marcus Bignot
Michael Moore
**Physiotherapy Staff:**
Steve Shipway:
Pam Hodgetts

# History

*b*ristol City Women's Football history dates back to 1990, when Bristol City FC's first community officer Shaun Parker and his assistant Richard Wilson took on the responsibility of developing Women's Football at Ashton Gate. Contact was made with a team called Bristol United who played a series of friendly matches at Brislington School but who had no affiliation with the professional football club beyond being supporters. Rachel McArthur, who rejoined the ladies team this year following spells at Southampton Saints and Fulham, is the sole player remaining from the original senior squad. They were invited to represent Bristol City FC and were provided with kit, a space in the programme and appearances on the pitch in an effort to develop and advertise the women's game. In the early days there was a sense of excitement and a feeling of creating history, although it was not without its critics. As a result of the new partnership, the club's women's football scene gained momentum, and by 1994 the club had formed two senior sides and embraced two football-loving fathers, Roger Bowyer and Andy Bayliss, who together with twelve young girls had formed three junior sides playing in an indoor 6-a-side league at Whitchurch Sports Centre in Bristol on a Sunday morning.

These two people must be credited with the present club's inception and it is testimony to their achievements that many of the youngsters who joined in that era are regulars in this year's National Division side. History was made for the club in 1994 when the women's senior team appeared in the Women's FA Cup Semi-Final versus Liverpool. The event received huge regional media coverage and attracted a crowd of over two thousand at Mangotsfield Town, which was unheard of in those days. Despite a 5-0 defeat, it really put the club on the map. In the 2004-2005 season, the club runs two senior teams and u16, u14, u12 and u10 teams coached through the Bristol City Centre of Excellence under the guidance of A license coach Ian Tincknell. The first team, having won the South West Combination League title in 2001-2002 and finished runners up to Bristol Rovers in the Gloucestershire Challenge Cup between 1998 and 2001, were promoted into the Premier League Southern Division for the first time in 2002. Finishing in third place in their first season, and having the same points as the second-placed team, was an excellent achievement. Determination and hard work has seen the team become stronger and more fearless when taking on higher opposition. In the 2003-2004 season the team were unbeaten in their opening sixteen League matches, winning fourteen of them including a crunch meeting with title rivals Southampton Saints. Their hard work, confidence and never-say-die attitude culminated in promotion to the highly coveted National Division for the 2004-2005 sea-

son under previous manager Jack Edgar. To cap a perfect season off, they beat local rivals Bristol Rovers in the Gloucestershire Challenge Cup for the first time in five years. To add to this success, the club's Women's section Chairman Nick King received the Nationwide Marketing Award for 2003-2004 at the Awards ceremony in London in May 2004, having worked hard to raise the profile of the team and market the club in such a way that a big improvement was seen in match day attendances which averaged over one hundred and seventy five for League games. At the same awards, Charlotte King was awarded the Top Goalscorer award for the Southern Division, although she was actually the highest scorer of the entire Premier League with twenty one League goals ahead of fellow team-mate Angie Tinson who came third in the Southern Division. The 2004-2005 season saw Pete Amos take charge of the senior team after disappointing results at the start of the National Division programme. A former England u18s schoolboy's coach, Pete also runs the Bristol City FA Academy u16 team and is Assistant Director of the Bristol City Boy's FA Academy. The role was Pete's first in Women's Football, although he is well known to a number of the City players having worked with several of them at the Academy. Pete's first game in charge was a tough Premier League Cup match at high flying Southern Division table topping Chelsea where the team ensured Pete's first match in charge of City Women ended in a 2-1 win after extra time! Hard-working Assistant Coach for the first team is Wayne Roberts a Sports Development Officer at Bath University, who also assists with the Team Bath Ladies.

The reserve team under Manager Andy Bray played in the South West Women's League in season 2002-2003, before joining the National Reserve League in the 2003-2004 season, finishing midway with twenty four points, having drawn the most amount of games of any team in their division. At the time of writing, the

reserve team are on course for promotion into the Southern Division 1. Bill Meehan joined as reserve coach to assist Andy for the 2004-2005 season to further strengthen the coaching pool at the club.

The club has enjoyed much success over the years, winning many tournaments, competitions, League titles and Fair Play awards. Much of their development in the 11-a-side game took place in Wales as they were the only League to run full sided games at that time. We have had a number of Gloucestershire, Somerset and Wiltshire County players in our squads with several members having attended England trials in the past. Jade Bailey has attended u15 and u17 training camps, young Kate Roberts has gained selection for the Welsh u17 and u19 squads. Darel Poole and Laura Niblett attend England u19 training sessions with Darel having gained five England u17 caps and three u19 caps and was Captain in all five of her u17 appearances. Rachel McArthur, our newest star signing for 2004-2005, is also a member of the England Senior Squad. Rachel was the first, and only, Bristol-born player to achieve this prestigious honour.

In the 2001-02 season, Bristol City Women's FC became the first FA Charter Standard Club in the area, male or female, with two members of the committee Patrick and Ann Bevan (General Manager and Secretary), receiving awards from the County FA in recognition of their significant contribution to football. In 2003, the women's section of the club was fully integrated with the boys FA Licensed Academy. The girls' Academy programme mirrors the boy's work both in football terms and educationally, with courses taylor-made to suit each player's academic ability. The Academy is now based at the new state-of-the-art City Academy in St George, Bristol.

Photographs courtesy of Keith Fowler

## Bristol City WFC
## Who's Who

**President -** Maggie Lansdown
**Chairman** - Nick King
**First Team Manager** - Pete Amos
**Reserve Team Manager** - Andy Bray

# History

bristol Rovers Women's Football Club was formed as a senior club in 1998. Prior to that, the players, consisting of under-16s, had been trained by their fathers in the local park. They played a few 11-a-side games and took part in a 6-a-side league. In that same season, the team joined forces with Cable-Tel LFC. As both clubs were looking to promote women's football in the region, they approached Bristol Rovers FC to use the club name. As a result, the two clubs merged together and founded Bristol Rovers Women's Football Club.

A second team was also formed playing their football in the South West Women's League. The first two seasons saw Rovers finish second in the League by just a single point, just missing out in their quest for Premier League status. Season 2000/01 proved to be a memorable one for Rovers, winning the South West Women's Combination League with an unbeaten record and clinching promotion to the Southern Division of the FAWPL. In the same year Rovers embarked on a tremendous cup run, reaching the Semi-Finals of the WFA Cup, where they took on Arsenal Ladies at the Memorial Stadium, losing 3-0 in front of a crowd in excess of three thousand. That same year Rovers completed a hat trick GFA Women's Challenge Cup victories.

2002-03 saw not only a change in League status but also in the team management with Tony Ricketts taking over from Dave Bell in the 'hot-seat'. That season, the club finished second in the Southern Division to run-away leaders, Fulham. During the summer of 2003, the squad was virtually rebuilt for the following season and this included a significant change in playing status. Rovers took a professional step forward with the financial backing of the parent club as well as Filton College, who became principal sponsors.

Close links were set up so young players could combine their education whilst still continuing to develop their football skills in the Bristol Academy of Sport.

The first season as a semi-professional team saw much success on the field. Not only did the GasGirls clinch promotion to the National Division with a quarter of the games still remaining, but also made the quarter-finals of the league cup and the semi finals of the WFA Cup. Last season proved to be a hard challenge. The GasGirls had to continually fight a battle against relegation in this their first season in the top flight. They eventually survived by a mere five points to ensure Premier League status for the following season.

The highlight of the season was making the semi-finals of the F.A. for the third time in four years before finally losing to Arsenal once again, 2-0 in a tightly contested match. This season has seen yet more changes, with Gary Green taking over the reins as Manager and with Claire Scanlan, the Irish International signed from Leeds, as his assistant.

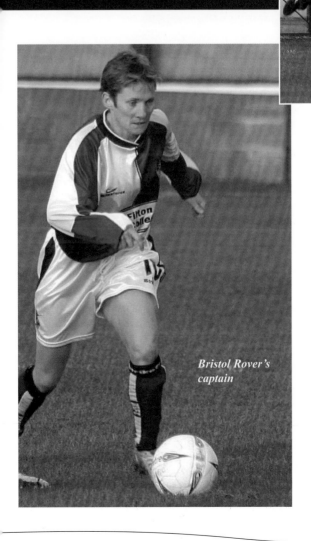

*Bristol Rover's captain*

# History

Charlton Athletic's first team plays in the National Division of the FA Nationwide Premier League - the top flight of women's football in England. The Addicks finished in third place in the 2000/01 and 2001/02 seasons, and fourth in 2002/03, and having led the League for much of the following campaign, missed out on the title in the last game of last season, ultimately finishing as runners-up. Charlton were formed in 2000, when Croydon, who had won the League title and lifted the FA Cup the previous season, came under the umbrella of the Addicks. The club immediately lifted its first trophy following a draw with Arsenal Ladies in August of that year in the Charity Shield - with both clubs sharing the trophy following the 1-1 result, and with Emily Arnold scoring

*Addicks striker Katie Chapman in action*

the goal. Manager Gill Wylie left the club midway though the 2000/01 campaign, and was replaced by Keith Boanas, who was then manager of the Ryman League Tooting and Mitcham men's team. Boanas led the club to the semi-final of the Premier League Cup in his first season and Charlton also won the London Cup, competed for by a mixture of the first-team and reserve side in April 2003. One of the highlights of the club's achievement in its short existence, however, was reaching the FA Cup final the following month. More than ten thousand fans flocked to Selhurst Park to watch Charlton take on treble chasing Fulham in the final, with over two million people also tuning in to see the

game live on the BBC. Unfortunately the Addicks lost 3-0, and it was an identical scoreline, albeit to Arsenal, when Charlton reached the final stage again in May 2004. This time the match was played at Loftus Road. By that stage of the season Charlton had already tasted trophy success, however, having beaten Fulham to lift the Premier League Cup following a 1-0 win at Barnet's Underhill Stadium. The hero that day in March was Emma Coss, who scored with a header from a corner just minutes after coming off the bench to replace injured captain Casey Stoney. Charlton's reserves compete in the National Reserve League South, Division One. They finished second in the 2001/02 season, and won the Kent County Cup in May 2003, beating Millwall 3-1 at Bromley FC.

# Behind the Scenes

*t*he women's team enjoys all of the resources the club can provide - from training facilities, full kit, transport, match pitches, sports science and medical support, to full administration, media and secretarial support, hospitality and a well-structured management committee. The club has also announced the biggest sponsorship deal in women's football when a three-year deal with Berkshire-based management consultancy firm Footdown was agreed in 2001. Charlton also run the successful Charlton's Women's Football Academy, with first-team manager Keith Boanas also acting as the director of the Academy and Centre of Excellence. Together with integration into the club, this provides the team with an excellent structure and a great foundation for the future. Eighteen girls have progressed from Charlton's Centre of Excellence and Academy programmes to the senior squad, where they compete for a place in the first team with a host of England internationals. Training is held at Charlton's first-class training ground at Sparrows Lane in New Eltham. Home games were played at Bromley's Hayes Lane ground for the two previous seasons, and the female Addicks have played at Sparrows Lane as well. In 2003/04 the club formed a Women's Football Board to oversee the running of the female Charlton team.

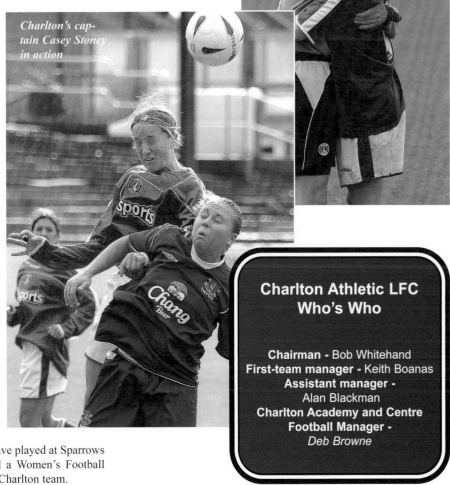

*Charlton's captain Casey Stoney in action*

## Charlton Athletic LFC Who's Who

**Chairman** - Bob Whitehand
**First-team manager** - Keith Boanas
**Assistant manager** -
Alan Blackman
**Charlton Academy and Centre
Football Manager** -
*Deb Browne*

# History

Originally founded in 1969 as the Belle Vue Ladies by young women who were selling draw tickets on the terraces at Doncaster Rovers, the club started out by playing local small-sided games, but within a short period of time found they were venturing outside of Doncaster. where the Belle Vue part of the name had no meaning, and so in 1971 they changed their name and became Doncaster Belles! After Championship success in the regional leagues (twelve out of thirteen in the Notts League and two out of two in the North East League), in addition to many tournaments and Cup successes, the Belles became fonder members of the National League in the 1991/92 season, where they completed the League and FA Cup double without conceding a game! In the seven year history of the National League set-up, Doncaster Belles completed the double once more, and in this Championship have finished second four times and third twice. Away from the major trophies for the past four years, the Belles' 1998/99 pre-season preparation included participation in the prestigious Reebok Tournament, which they won for the third time. More recently the Club has also been strengthened by a number of senior signings and by the promotion of some of last year's young regional players. In 2001 we were runners up in both the F.A cup and the Women's Premier league. Last season we were again successful in the league finishing runners up to Fulham. We are now in our second year of a major sponsorship with Green Flag which will enable us to continue our development at both senior and junior levels.

DONCASTER ROVER BELLES

### Doncaster Rover Belles
Who's Who

**Chairman -** John Gomersall

**Head of Coaching -** John Buckley

**Club Secretary -** Nigel Hyde

**President -** Shiela Edmunds

**Everton**

# History

everton Ladies was formed originally as a five-a-side team known as Dolphins Youth and this ran from Birkenhead Youth Club. The development of an 11 a side team came later along with the adoption of a local sponsors name Leasowe Pacific. The team

dominated the North West Women's League and Cup competitions throughout the 80s and early 90s. In 1988 they were runners up to the famous Doncaster Belles in their first FA Cup Final. Their successful 1989 Final against Friends of Fulham was the first ever televised Women's FA Cup Final. The build-up and the game itself had full coverage from Channel 4. This programme helped raise the profile of women's football both in Merseyside and throughout England. Following their FA Cup success, the team represented English Football in an International tournament hosted by AC Milan on the beautiful island of Sardinia. This proved to be a magnificent experience and their first introduction to European Football. 1994 saw the merge of Leasowe Pacific and Everton Football and their first season in the Premier League. Their first achievements under the Everton banner came in season 1996/1997 when they reached the final of the League Cup v Millwall Lionesses - runners up. During season 1997/1998, they won the FA Premier League. Following this the most memorable occasion was when the league trophy was presented at Goodison Park in front of a crowd numbering thirty five thousand!

A Charity Shield match V Arsenal was played on the 'hallowed turf' at Wembley, prior to the men's Arsenal v Manchester United Charity Shield. Further achievements came in 2000 when the club reached the League Cup Final at Tranmere Rovers this time losing out to Arsenal! From 2000 to 2005 the focus has been the development of the youth section and Centre of Excellence programme. This had to be the focus, with several key players departing for professional or semi professional football. The FA Centre of Excellence has been established since 2001and during this period, over fifteen players have progressed through to England training camps. Many of the u16s Centre of Excellence players progressed through to Everton Ladies First Team and helped the club retain Premiership status in 2003. The youth section has been the foundation of the club and we now boast several teams from: u8, u10, u12,u14, u16,a youth team, reserve team and the first team. Everton has one of the largest and strongest female sections throughout the country and are one of few teams to have played every season since their introduction to the FA Premier League. Season 2005 has seen a huge turn around and consistent performances have seen Everton in the top three in the League, all season and an FA Cup Final place after beating Arsenal 3-0 in the Semi Final and breaking their unbeaten record.

# Mo Marley - A Manager's Story

my first introduction to women's football came at the age of ten . My two elder sisters played for a 'Metal Box' where we lived in Speke. I often attending training sessions and as soon as I was old enough I participated in games. My first competitive game was for Connah's Quay Nomads as by this team the team Metal box had folded. Most of the players were grown women, as each team only had an open age team as there was no youth structure in place. I continued to play for this team until I was sixteen years old, then I took a year out as I was constantly having battles about wether girl's should play football or not. Several of my friends had no interest in football therefore I was a little distracted. From 17-19 I played for Daresbury Ladies and I enjoyed my playing career again. I watched Leasowe Pacific in 1987 and signed relishing the challenge of playing higher standard football.

1989 I played at Old Trafford in the FA Cup Final - the first game to be shown on television. - Winner
1989 International Tournament - Sardinia
1997 League Cup Final v Millwall - Runners up
1997/1998 Premier League Champion
1998 Charity Shield at Wembley (Lost on penalties to Arsenal)
2000 League Cup Final at Tranmere (Lost to Arsenal)
1995 First England Cap - Croatia
2001 Captained England to European Championship - Germany
1998 and until the present day England u19 Coach - 2 European Championship Finals Stages and World Cup quarter finalist.
1998 -2005 Football Development Officer - Liverpool County FA.
2003 Achieved UEFA A License Coaching Award
2003 Everton Ladies First Team Manager
2005 and until the present date Everton Football Club Women and Girls Football Development Officer

I was formerly employed as a pay roll clerk in Liverpool but with the demands of International commitments as a player the relationship with my former employer was strained so I resigned from my job in April 1998. It was convenient for me as this allowed me to train without the demands of a full time job. In September 1998 I applied for a part time position as a Women and girls Football Development Officer with the Liverpool County FA and I was appointed in September 1998. Part time work and the full support of the County to release me to play and coach at International level was major factor in helping me sustain all roles. Throughout my playing career I played for Everton from 1987 until 2004 and then progressed to Team Manager and Coach. The position of coach /manager was to help me attain the A License coaching badge. I have forty two England Caps (several as captain) and played my first game for England at the age of twenty eight, about three weeks after getting married. I intended on retiring at the end of that season to start a family but my International career put all that on hold. During my employment as the development officer for Liverpool County FA I had the pleasure of establishing programmes to help you female players participate and enjoy the game. Introduction of sessions in schools was pleasing and went back to my old school to deliver a session. We created clear pathways for talented per-

formers. All this was important to me as when I was younger there was nothing in place and I could very well have missed out on the wonderful experiences football has given me. In March 2005, I was appointed Women and Girls Football Development Officer for Everton Football Club. This is a major progression for the club and women and girls football in general. This will help forge better links for the Ladies Elite teams and provide clear pathways from community projects.

**Everton LFC**
**Who's Who**

**Chairwoman and Manager -**
Mo Marley

**Assistant Coach and Sport's Scientist -** Andy Spence

**Secretary -** Kate McCann

**Physiotherapist -** Amanda Li

# History

*f*ulham Ladies has led the way in the development of women's football over the last ten years - a sport that now attracts more women and girls than any other. Fulham Ladies FC has won every domestic honour available and competed in European competitions. A period of professional status ended in 2003 and the team, under the management of Marieanne Spacey, now compete as semi-professionals. Last season, 2003-2004, Marieanne's first in charge, saw the team win the Community Shield, progress to the Premier League Cup Final, where they lost by a goal to Charlton Athletic, and a League campaign that went all the way to the wire, culminating in a three-way battle between Charlton, Arsenal and Fulham. In front of several thousand spectators at Highbury, Fulham narrowly missed out on their second consecutive National Premier Division title when they lost to the Gunners in the final game of the 2003/4 season. Fulham competed in the UEFA Women's cup during season 2003-2004 and reached the quarter finals, losing out to FC Frankfurt, a team made up predominantly of German international players. Fulham LFC is one of the biggest names in women's football and attracts a strong match day following from supporters of the club. This season, 2004-2005, has seen many changes at the club, several of the team's more experienced players left in the Summer and Spacey has replaced them with a host of young and talented junior internationals. The side has taken time to bond, and results have not always gone their way, but the side is one that will develop over coming years and reap rewards in seasons to come. The club kept the services of Leanne Hall, Jess Wright and Corinne Yorston, all experienced England Internationals at varying age groups, for season 2004-2005, and these players have been instrumental in the first season of the development plan that has

been set out over the next three seasons. Fulham Ladies Football Club is not just about the first team. Growing the game at grass-roots is equally as important. The club has a Centre of Excellence for girls from the age of ten to sixteen, has recently opened an Academy at a local college to encourage young women to continue playing whilst undertaking higher education, and it also runs girls-only soccer coaching through seven Boroughs in London and Surrey. These players are all aware that there is a pathway for them to reach First team football at the club. Girls can start at Fulham as part of a Community Soccer Course, progress through the Development Centre onto the Centre of Excellence into the Academy and then into senior women's football at reserve or first team level. Women's football is very much a family affair; it attracts a wide audience of men, women and children. Spectator numbers vary from several hundred a week for Premier League games to several thousand for big cup games. Marieanne Spacey is probably the most famous name in women's football in

the UK. She has over ninety one caps, played in seven European Championships, and during her ten- year career with Arsenal, won no less than four Premier League titles, four FA Cups and five Premier League Cups. Fulham Ladies are one of a growing number of women's teams that receive support from the professional men's club. The Chairman, Mohamed Al Fayed, has always been very supportive of the women's set-up and continues to be. The Board at FFC are also very supportive and attend games as spectators on occasions.

## Fulham LFC
## Who's Who

**Chairman**: Mohamed Al Fayed
**Manager**: Marieanne Spacey
**Head of Community**:
Simon Morgan
**Physio**: Gemma Davies

*Marieanne Spacey in commanding role*

# History

Leeds United Ladies was formed in 1989 by community coaches Cess Podd and Dick Wright. They set up one team of mixed age and ability players. After seven seasons playing in the Yorkshire and Humberside League, the season 1997/98 saw the first team gain promotion to the AXA FA Northern Premier League. The pinnacle of the club's success being season 2001-2001, achieving the champions position of the Northern Premier League and promotion to the National Women's Premier League. The club won the honour being voted Northern Club of the Year for two years in succession and gained recognition for its Volunteer Investment Programme receiving a Highly Commended Certificate for the North East Area of Sport England. We are a FA Chartermark Club. Football within the club is lead by a Director of Football who works with all the team managers to ensure consistency of development and welfare for all our girls. The coaching staff is made up of FA qualified coaches. Over the years the club has evolved to three open age teams, one of them being a development team for talented Under 19 players, and six junior teams, ranging from under 10s to under 16s. We currently have eighty youth players, and a squad of fifty open age players. We have a qualified Club Chartered Physiotherapist available to all players for injury diagnosis and treatment where appropriate and a qualified Sports Scientist to assist. We are a Club developing and expanding and looking forward to the challenges of the future.

*Julie Chipchase in thoughtful mood*

*Leeds and England International Sue Smith in action*

**Leeds United LFC
Who's who**

**General Manager -** Melanie Vauvelle
**First Team Manager -** Julie Chipchase
**Reserve Team Manager -**
Martin Fogarty
**Club Physiotherapist -**
Rebecca Wade

# History

*t*he club was formed under the name of Newton Ladies in 1989. In order to become affiliated to the first National League, the club changed its name to Knowsley WFC in 1991, finishing fourth in the league. During the summer of 1992, the club strengthened its squad with the addition of a number of England internationals. The 1992/93 season saw the club finish third in the league and make its only appearance at Wembley stadium in the league cup final, losing to Arsenal. The 1993/94 season saw the first of three successive appearances in the F.A. Cup Final, losing 1-0 to Doncaster Belles and finishing third in the league. In time for the following season, the club changed its name to Liverpool F.C. Ladies, with the full support of the Liverpool F.C. men's club. However the first honour once again proved elusive as the club finished runners up in both the league and F.A. Cup. In the 1996/7, 1997/8 and 1998/9 seasons, the club finished in a comfortable mid table position. Whilst several experienced players remained it was becoming clear that the lack of investment in a youth/reserve set up in the mid 1990's had resulted in the club falling behind its rivals at both national and local level, as Liverpool were one of the few National League teams with no youth development programme. The 1999/00 season saw the start of the plan to put this right with the incorporation of Liverpool Feds Juniors. A double cup success at Under10 level being the first of hopefully many honours. Season 2003/04 has seen the youth teams all ending their seasons extremely well with the Under 12s C and A, and the Under 14s winning silverware. The club

now has a very strong youth structure the future of Liverpool FC Ladies looks bright. The excellent support from Liverpool Football Club continues today with the links growing stronger by the season, in securing a 'kit' sponsorship with Reebok and with the financial backing from Liverpool Football Club along with Carlsberg means the ladies can concentrate on winning the league and cups. The 2002/03 season saw the Liverpool FC Ladies reserve team finish runners up in Division 2 which won them promotion into the National Premiership Reserve Division. This season Liverpool FC Ladies have had their best season ever in the league, winning the Northern Premiership and remaining unbeaten throughout --the first Liverpool FC team to do this since 1892. The competitive season ended with the County cup final and an early test against

National League opposition in the form of Everton Ladies. This was a hard-fought game at Anfield which went to penalties, Liverpool FC Ladies beat Everton 4-3. Liverpool FC Ladies are off on tour to Singapore followed by a tournament in Ireland. these are exciting times as the reds keep marching on.

### Singapore trip May 2004
The club has developed strong links with James Lim, a Singapore businessman and full time Liverpool fan. In 2004, the squad flew out to Singapore on their first tour of the Far East. Comprising of friendly matches, and the provision of training sessions for local under privileged children, it proved a huge success and a return trip is penciled in for summer 2005.

### Ireland Tournament 2004
The club also took part in a tournament which is held in Carrick Fergus, Northern Ireland each year in the close season. This tournament sees a number of teams taking part for the honour of wining the P&O Trophy.

# Training

*l*iverpool FC Ladies train twice a week, on Tuesdays. They are usually found at St Edwards School, Liverpool. This session is used for fitness training and sometimes they go to a local gym for spinning lessons. On fridays, training is held at the state-of - the art LFC Academy in Kirby, which has produced such players as Michael Owen, and Steven Gerrard.

## Liverpool LFC Who's Who

Chairman: Eddie Sinnott
Manager: John Williams
Coach: Craig Boyd
Coach: Greg Murphy
Physio: Mark Veidmen
Physio: Ewan Simpson

# The Northern Division

 **Aston Villa LFC**

 **Blackburn Rovers LFC**

 **Coventry City LFC**

 **Lincoln City LFC**

 **Manchester City LFC**

 **Middlesbrough LFC**

 **Oldham Curzon LFC**

 **Sunderland LFC**

 **Stockport County LFC**

 **Sheffield Wednesday LFC**

 **Tranmere Rovers LFC**

 **Wolverhampton Wanderers WFC**

# History

the Club was originally formed in the late 1970s as Solihull LFC. The Club had several successful seasons in the Midland League, regularly winning the League Championship and various cup competitions. In 1988, they reached the quarter-finals of The Women's FA Cup, narrowly losing to Millwall. In 1989 Solihull responded to an advert from Aston Villa Football Club requesting help to form a ladies team. The name of the Club was changed to Aston Aztecs and a relationship with Aston Villa was forged and the Club became the officially recognised ladies team of Aston Villa. The season 1989-1990 also saw the introduction of a second team with junior teams at under sixteen and under thirteen introduced in 1991. Over the next five years, the club continued to prosper both on and off the pitch. The Roll of Honour displays considerable success for all squads. In 1996, the club agreed once again to change its name to become fully recognised as the ladies team representing Aston Villa Football Club. From 1998-99, the Senior Team won promotion to the National Division of The FA Women's Premier League. The 2000-01 season saw the introduction of an under 10s team to provide a good standard of football and training for talented young girls. The club currently has a first and reserve team at all levels from under 12 level to seniors, with a single team at under 10 level. The club's coaches are also an

integral part of The Aston Villa Girls Centre of Excellence which aims to develop talented girl footballers. The club has also worked hard to develop further, with the junior and senior section achieving The FA Charter Standard. Additionally two of the coaches winning the Birmingham County FA Junior Coach of the Year in consecutive years. The club has continued to forge closer links with Aston Villa FC, and with the kind support of Mr Doug Ellis and Dave Ismay, will continue to promote the Claret and Blue in the ladies game.

### Aston Villa LFC
### Who's Who

**Chairman -** Steve Fisher
**First Team Manager -** Terry Unitt
**Reserve Team Manager -**
Andy Mulligan
**Patron -** Emma B of Radio 1

# Season 2003 - 2004

t his last season has been one of the toughest yet one of the most productive seasons for the ladies team. Under a new management team Andrew McNally (Manager) and Marek Walsh (Assistant Manager) the ladies have not only won the northern Combination League they completed a double by winning the Lancashire Cup. The ladies won the Northern Combination with a 100% record, beating top teams home and away such as Manchester United, Newcastle United, East Durham, Blackpool, and Chester City. Newcastle and East Durham Away games being two of the toughest going 2 - 0 down to East Durham to wining 3 - 2 at full time. The Lancashire Cup campaign was never going to be easy with ten quality teams entering this year's cup. Our first knock out round was Manchester United away which is never an easy task, but the ladies pulled through a 2 - 0 win to see us play lower division Hopwood in the next round. Hopwood found the fantastic Academy pitches overwhelming and succumbed to an 8 - 0 defeat. We went on to face a strengthened Blackpool team and a late equaliser from Blackpool made it 1 -1 after injury time, and our ladies settled the Semi final on Penalties and beat Blackpool 4 - 2. The final was to be held at the County ground and our opponents were Preston North End who had just successfully gained promotion from the regional leagues. The game was hard fought but after forty five minutes, Blackburn were in control and won 4 - 2.

# Season 2004 - 2005

anager Andrew McNally knew the Northern Premier was a big step up from the Combination Leagues. This season for the club it was all about consolidating a top half position and looking to retain the Lancashire cup whilst rebuilding a team for the next season to challenge for championship. Andrew McNally knew that to keep the club healthy and to strive forward as a team and a club he would have to make big decisions. Only five players were fielded at the end of this season that picked up the trophies last season. However the club has made a massive impact on this League being the only team to beat Sunderland twice, and until now losing the fewest games in the league, and finishing in the top four. As a club the progress we have made has been down to a fantastic management team alongside a huge scouting network and signing top established players with some of the best youth players in the North.

Blackburn Rovers have amazingly reached the Lancashire Cup final for the second year running and will face league rivals Oldham Curzon. A great run beating Preston, Blackpool and Manchester United has given Andrew and the club another chance of silverware. As you can see this has been the hardest route to the final and all credit to the players who have put in some great performances to get there. For the first year Blackburn Rovers have fielded a reserve team under the management of Adam Lakeland. The reserves have had a mixed set of results as you would expect. However for its first year it has managed to supply the fist team with three players and no few than six reserves have made senior debuts. All in all a productive season for the reserves.

Blackburn Rovers LFC
Who's Who

**Chairman** - Anthony Barlow

**Manager** - Andrew McNally

**Assistant Manager and Secretary** -
Marek Walsh

**Physiotherapist** - Steve Watson

# History

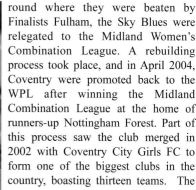

Coventry City Ladies FC was founded in 1991, although various Coventry Ladies sides were playing as long ago as 1910. The present club started in the West Midlands Regional League, and won the League in 1995-96 but lost in the Premier League play-offs to Calverton MW. The 1996-1997 season saw Coventry City win the West Midlands League and finish unbeaten, beating both Calverton MW and Middlesbrough 1-0 to secure promotion to the FA Women's Premier League

round where they were beaten by Finalists Fulham, the Sky Blues were relegated to the Midland Women's Combination League. A rebuilding process took place, and in April 2004, Coventry were promoted back to the WPL after winning the Midland Combination League at the home of runners-up Nottingham Forest. Part of this process saw the club merged in 2002 with Coventry City Girls FC to form one of the biggest clubs in the country, boasting thirteen teams. The

club has now received the FA's Charter Standard Award. This season, the club moved to Coventry Sphinx FC in order to meet FA ground criteria and finished as runners up in the Birmingham County FA Cup, recording a club record, with an 11-0 away victory at Leamington, beating Rugby 9-0, Bustleholme 9-1, and West Bromwich Albion 7-1 away, before losing to cup holders Birmingham City 3-1 in extra time in the final at the Birmingham County FA HQ. Another facet has been a successful awareness programme aimed at supporters of Coventry City's men's teams to get them interested in the club and its activities, and this season, we have enlisted the Coventry support news service to help us keep Coventry supporters informed. Previous managers include Neil Chatterton, Simon Benn, John Neeson, Dave Cartwright, Paul Barnes and Neil Wilson.

whilst also winning the Regional and League Cup. The Sky Blues had five seasons in the AXA Women's Premier League Northern Division, boasting excellent links with the Coventry City Centre of Excellence, Henley College Academy and Coventry City FC. However, 2001-2002 was not a good season. Despite a run to the FA Cup fifth

# Coventry City LFC
## Who's Who

**President -** Brian Ellis

**Chairman -** Dave Singleton

**Vice Chairman -** Martin Igoe

**Head Coach -** Mark Phillips

**Assistant Coach -** Ian Weaving

# History

## Six Promotions in Seven Years

*I*ncoln City Ladies was formed in 1995, as an under 16s Girls' Team by Football in the Community's Stuart Donnelly. The first season was spent in the Notts League before moving to the Unibond East Midlands League in 1996. Also that year Glen Harris started an additional under 14s team and Andy Hewitt an under 12s team. The girls were promoted to Division Two in 1997 and Division One the following season. Also in 1998 it was decided that the 1st Team should now lose its junior status and for the first time, became known as Lincoln City Ladies. Promotion to the Unibond East Midlands Premier Division came in 1999. Under the FITC umbrella, Stuart Donnelly and Liz Davies started the Lincoln City Ladies School of Excellence. In 2000-2001, Glen Harris took over as First Team Manager and Andy Hewitt formed a reserve side. The first team again won promotion to the Midland Combination. 2001-2002 was a momentous season for the ladies. Not only did they win the Midlands Combination but also attracted a gate of over one thousand eight hundred to Sincil Bank to see a Women's FA Cup Game against Everton. The promotion to the National League was celebrated with an open top bus ride through the City to a Civic reception given by the Mayor at the Guildhall. The Girls had gained six promotions in seven years. In the 2002 to 2003 Season, Lincoln broke a number of records in their first season in the National League. Lincoln was the first Ladies Team to play all their home fixtures at a League Ground, Sincil Bank, and attracted the highest total attendances over a league campaign. They also broke the Northern Premier attendance for a league match with a record with one thousand five hundred spectators watching the

Lady Imps play Oldham after a Firework Spectacular. In the Women's FA Cup the Ladies reached the quarter finals, going out 3-1 to Bristol Rovers. Lincoln won the County Cup, for the first time, beating five times winners Scunthorpe Utd. In 2003 to 2004 the Lady Imps consolidated their position in the Northern Premier and again beat Scunthorpe Ladies in the County Cup Final. Their achievement in developing young talent was recognised by having three players selected for the England Youth Teams, Katie Holtham, Lee Cobham and Nick Hobbs. In 2004, Glen Harris resigned as Manager and Rod Wilson, Glen's assistant took over. Ellie Gilliett was selected for England under 17s carrying on the legacy of Youth Development at the Club. As interest has grown over the years and the younger players have matured, more teams have been formed. There are currently seven teams in the group: under 10s, u12s, u14s, u61s, u18s, the reserves and the first team. Many present members of the senior sides joined when or shortly after the ladies first formed. These include Megan Harris, Karen Burton, Stacy Aisthorpe, Shelly Futter, Sara Priestly, Tracy Duxbury, Sarah Kennedy and Jess Maclean. The Lady Imps have a three year plan to continue to develop the club. In 2004 the Ladies Team took the initial steps to semi-professional status and it is the club's intention to expand upon these lines to enable the team to eventually gain promotion to the Premiere League. This year Lincoln College is starting a Ladies Academy for under 19s girls to study while receiving expert coaching. It is proposed that by linking up with the Lincoln University this will eventually form part of a full status Academy where girls can go on to complete their degrees or vocational studies.

**Lincoln City LFC
Who's Who**

**Chairman -**
Rick Futter
**1st team Manager/Coach -**
Rod Wilson
**Assistant 1st team Coach -**
Lee Armstrong
**Reserve Team Manager -**
Andy Scurr

# History

manchester City Ladies was formed in 1987, officially affiliating to the FA and League in 1989. In this time, the club has grown to become one of the top ladies football clubs in the country, with over one hundred and thirty players playing at all levels from the age of nine, picking up honours at all levels on a regular basis. The club has an excellent relationship with Manchester City FC and receives tremendous financial support, as well as invaluable assistance, access to new kit, fund raising and development activities. In addition, the parent club provides venues for Committee Meetings, Annual General Meetings and Presentation Evenings at the City of Manchester Stadium. The club is managed by a Club Committee and all team managers and coaches are qualified to the National FA level in coaching, child protection and first aid. All club officials have successfully completed the FA CRB registration in recent months. This group of volunteers give up a great deal of their time and energy to ensure the club is run in a professional manner. In December 2003 the club achieved The FA Charter Standard Club award for both junior and adult sections.

Manchester City Ladies has its own well designed and administered website www.mancityladies.com, providing further proof that the club is forging ahead in the development and promotion of girls' and women's football. All this makes us a very popular choice for new players looking for a safe, friendly, ambitious, forward thinking club, operating in a professional manner. The club is constantly searching for new players to strengthen the teams and take the club to the next level, which we hope will be:

1. The first team playing in the Nationwide Premier League National Division by season 2008/9.
2. The club being further recognised as the centre of excellence at all levels for girls' and women's football in the Greater Manchester area.

To help achieve these goals the club has this year become more focused on fund raising and has raised over fifteen thousand pounds through donations, fund raising events and benefits in kind from Manchester City FC. In addition to coverage in the local press, the club enjoys promotion from Manchester City FC, featuring regularly in match programmes and monthly supporters magazines. Joint initiatives are underway to help achieve the club's aims and promote women's football alongside the name of Manchester City FC. The club further benefits from access to top quality UEFA licensed coaching staff attached to Manchester City

FC, who play an active part in the promotion and development of women's football at all levels.

# Club Teams

the club has nine teams participating in local and national leagues, an increase of over 25% in the last two years. The teams range from u10s to u14s. This season the club took steps to re-organise the senior section in order to build a suitable platform on and off the park to progress to the National division by 2008/9. This resulted in a number of new players being given the opportunity to step up to Premier League football. Notable successes in this area have been Nikki Twohig, Caz Dixon, Gemma Horner, Natalie Thomas, Kimberly Janes and latterly Alex Merrill who have all adapted well and have become regulars in the team. Part of this re-structuring saw the club create a Development Team comprising a mixture of under 15 and 16s players, competing in the Cheshire and Manchester Women's League. This is designed to enable the up-and-coming players to get a taste of senior soccer in a highly competitive League, and the girls have exceeded all expectations. The under 14s, after their League and Cup double last year, stepped up to 11 a-side football, playing in the Lancashire Girls League, coming up against stronger sides in the North West. The under 13s, moving up to 7 a-side have improved tremendously over the last year, picking up several honours over the summer period, and they have now established their place in the League. With strong performances from both the under 12 and under 11 sections this year, it is Manchester City Ladies' youngest team, the under 10s who led the trophy haul with a superb start to the season by winning the pre-season Tameside Challenge Cup. With the addition of new players to the already skilful and talented team, they are indeed proving to be the "team to beat" this year. With their unbeaten record, they sit proudly at the top of the table .

The club is extremely fortunate to be able to train at the-purpose build football training establishment of Manchester City's Platt Lane Complex where we have access to full-size indoor and outdoor pitches of the latest technology. Access to City's Injury Assessment Clinics and physiotherapy services are also available for first team players.

## Manchester City LFC Who's Who

**Chairman -** Gary Moores
**Secretary** - Graeme McLeish
**Manager -** Dave Judge
**Physiotherapist -** Supplied by Manchester City F.C.

*Pictures courtesy of Ed Garvey*

# History

*f*ormed way back in 1976, Middlesbrough FC Ladies was originally known as Cleveland Spartans. Cleveland Spartans started off in The Northern and Hull League for one season, before moving into The Nottingham League - where they stayed for four years. They returned to The Northern Counties League for another seven years, where they enjoyed quite a bit of success with five championship wins, five league cup wins and five K.O. cup wins. In season 1988-89, they joined The Yorkshire and Humberside league, where they stayed until 1997. Their next move was into the more local Northern Women's League. They won the "treble" of League championship, League cup and knock-out cup, and automatic promotion to the Northern Women's Combination league in 1998. By this time the name Middlesbrough Ladies was theirs, and after four strong seasons in the combination League, they finally won promotion to the FA Women's Premier League Northern Division- after two runners-up spots in season 2001-2002. At the start of the 2002-2003 season, Middlesbrough Football Club officially "adopted" the ladies team, and they now play under the official name of Middlesbrough FC Ladies, and with this, much needed financial support was given. The club is also currently looking for further sponsorship. During its twenty eight year history the club has played in The Women's FA Cup Final in 1982, two semi-finals, and several quarter-finals. It also participated in the Pontins 5-a side competitions, winning three times out of five, and playing in two north v south finals, winning one and losing one.

More recently, the club had the honour and pleasure of actually playing at Wembley before the Boro v Chelsea FA Cup Final in 1997. In addition, they have played at MFC'S Riverside Stadium once, but are working on that to get even more appearances! The club is now just entering its third season in the FA Women's Premier League Northern Division. Although their first season saw the ladies fight against relegation, their second season of improved football ensured a mid table sixth position finish. Boro's main aim for this third season is to continue with the improving form. However a lot of hard work and determination will be required by everyone at the club to achieve a settled position in this League. Once established, the club can then build towards a top-three place in this League and then develop and improve form over the coming season's National Premier League and have the privilege of playing against the likes of Arsenal, Fulham and Charlton ladies

## Middlesbrough LFC
## Who's Who

**Chairman -** John Dinsdale

**Manager -** Marrie Wieczorek

**First team coach -** Paul Cutler

**Reserve team manager -** Trevor Wing

**First team fitness trainer -** Phil Ray

# History

*t*he club was formed in March 1988 as Oldham Athletic Ladies FC and formed part of the Football Community Scheme. Trials were held on the stadium, which at that time was an astro-turf surface, a far cry from today's more modern synthetic surfaces, and the team joined The North West Women's League in 1990. The club moved rapidly through the Leagues in the nineties and it was from their then junior set-up, that many of the present senior team have emerged. A number of honours came the way of the squad and two of the current playing members from those early days have been involved with the England set-up. Kelly Dean represented England at under-18s level, while Emma Gaynon a couple of years later, was in the stand-by squad.

This season goalkeeper Kay Hawke has represented England at under 21 level and has also attended a number of full squad training sessions. As members of the Lancashire County FA, the club participated in the inaugural Lancashire County FA Women's Cup in 1994/95, when they were runners-up. They appeared in the following four Finals, winning three of them, but since 1998/99 they have struggled to make an impression on the competition, until this season, when they will now play fellow FA Women's Premier League side Blackburn Rovers LFC in the Final. During their period as Oldham Athletic Ladies FC, there was little or no support from the town team and they also had difficulty in finding a permanent home in the Oldham Borough, having to move from one club to another throughout the seasons. In 1988 they found what has now become their home, when they moved out of Oldham into neighbouring Ashton-U-Lyne, Tameside, and to the home of Curzon Ashton FC. They continued to play under their original name and in season 1998/1999, they joined the newly formed Northern Combination League and finished a credible third to winners Bangor City Girls FC, and twelve months later they achieved their ambitions of Premier League football when they won the Combination Championship after starting the season with seventeen straight wins. Their race for the title was helped by prolific goal scorer Kelly Dean who recorded forty two goals that season, five less than the campaign of twelve months earlier.

While the club entered the unknown of the Premier League, they soon had people taking notice, ending their first season as runners-up to Leeds United, forcing them to go to the final game of the season to take the title. The Women's FA Cup was another area in which the team gained credit, and in season 2001/02 they reached the quarter-final round, losing out to National Division side Tranmere Rovers, reaching that stage after beating National Division side Southampton Saints away from home. Twelve month later they matched their FA Cup performance, but once again exiting the competition at the hands of a National Division side, this time Fulham, who at that time were a full-time professional outfit.

In terms of individual performances since joining the Premier League, this accolade must go to Kelly Dean. In the club's first season, she won the Golden Boot Award (season 2000/01) outright and has shared it on two other occasions since then. But perhaps the biggest accolade Kelly could have received was at the 2004/05 Presentation Awards Dinner, when she was named as the only player out-

them to engage the services of a Football Development Coach and part of their remit will be to assist with the development of an under 16s girl's side and they to take it one stage further with an under-14s side.

The current season has been a disappointment in terms of performance, with the club experiencing their worst ever position in the Premier League. No one can really say what has gone wrong, but there is a clear determination to put it right during the summer months.

## Oldham Curzon LFC Who's Who

**Chair** - Graham Shuttleworth

**Secretary and Manager -** David Ryan

**Physio -** Caroline Shockledge

side of the National Division to have been named in the top six players of that season.

The club also received a pleasant surprise at the Dinner, winning the inaugural Fair Play Award, something which everyone connected with the club could be rightly proud of. It was the advent of their move into the Premier League that brought about the change of name for the club. Having been made welcome at the home of Curzon Ashton, and with no interest being shown from within the borough of their birth, the team dropped the Athletic and took on Curzon, to become Oldham Curzon Ladies FC. This new name helped them retain what links they had with Oldham while recognising the support that Curzon Ashton FC had given them.

Since those days the links have become stronger and the team is now firmly part of Curzon Ashton FC. It's hoped that the move to the new Tameside Stadium, which the club will take over in June 2005, will enable the ladies section to prosper. With less than adequate facilities at the former ground to enable them to develop the ladies section of the club, the new facility should be a catalyst for the next generation of players, and this season they have developed links with Royton Girls, who's teams go from under-16s and younger.

From next season, training will take place at the stadium on the latest all-weather surface available on the market, and it's hoped that this, along with the overall new development, will be an added attraction to players looking to play at Premier League level. As part of their overall grant to the club, the Football Foundation have provided funds to enable

**STOCKPORT COUNTY LFC**

# History

S tockport Co. Ladies F.C was formed in 1990 following an initiative from the local authority, giving the opportunity for a number of girls to play and develop their sporting interest. The first decade saw a degree of success, when a restructuring of the Club saw a major change in its fortunes in the Season of 2000/01 The appointment of A licensed Coach Andy Lee as First Team Manager was a significant factor. The team achieved a notable 'double' of League Championship and County Cup victory in season 2002/03.

*Photograph courtesy of Stockport County LFC*

This was followed with an excellent achievement of third place in their first season of Premier league competition, retention of the County Cup and four players receiving National recognition. Off the field, a unit of dedicated support staff is in place to address other issues, regarding technical improvement, health, welfare and educational development. The Club has achieved both the F.A. Charter standard and F.A. Community Club awards.

**Stockport County LFC
Who's Who**

**Chairman -** Paul Walton
**Manager -** Andy Lee
**Physiotherapist -** Ann Guilfoyle
**Secretary -** Steve O'Connell

# S U N D E R L A N D   L F C

# History

*t*he Kestrels were formed in 1989 as a five-a-side team playing at the Cowgate Leisure Centre. They soon graduated to an eleven-a-side line up and won the Yorkshire & Humberside League Championship at their first attempt in 1989-90. The Cowgate Kestrels joined the newly formed National League a year later and have maintained their position as the premier team in the North East, playing in the Northern Division for the last nine seasons and almost gaining promotion in 1993-94. The club has had a relatively unsettled history having also been known as RTM Newcastle Kestrels and Blyth Spartans Kestrels, and last season receiving valuable assistance from East Durham and Houghall Community College. They will now be known as Sunderland AFC Women, but will retain the Kestrels moniker as their nickname. Having just missed out on promotion in 98/99 (Aston Villa were the victors) the club finally achieved its ambition by winning the AXA F.A.

Women's Premier League Northern Division title and a place in the top flight. A feat that was accomplished in some style. Only five points were dropped in a campaign which saw the team score ninety league goals and concede just twenty one. The top three goalscorers in the division were all Kestrels, with Melanie Reay picking up the Top Scorer in the Division During the summer, the top men's side and women's side in the North East made the logical and exciting step when they joined together to help ensure that the region continued to compete at the highest level in all areas of football. In their first season as Sunderland AFC Women and their first year in the top flight, the team recorded some good results and some bad as they learnt to adapt to the higher tempo and technical level of the top league. The real achievement was retaining their status, which they did with two impressive away wins at Southampton and Millwall.

Several players left during the summer of 2001 (US scholarships etc.) and combined with injuries to senior players the young and depleted squad struggled to turn their more consistent performances into the results and points needed. Sunderland finished the season occupying the bottom berth, but there was success at the club as the reserves walked away

with the title in the Northern/Midlands Reserve Section of the Premier League at their first attempt.

Last season saw Sunderland make a challenge for promotion and a return to the top flight. Although Melanie Reay again picked up joint top scorer in the Division, poor form at the beginning of the season meant that the Black Cats had to be satisfied with second spot. The reserves also finished second, but both teams have another year behind them and should again be challenging for honours.

### Sunderland LFC
### Who's Who

Chairlady  Gillian Barker

Secretary  Jacqueline Henderson

Manager  Mick Mulhern

# History

SWLFC were formed at the Star Inn Public House in Rotherham 1971 after a charity match between men and women at the pub. The team was initially named "Star Ladies". It wasn't long before the side joined the Sheffield Ladies League, and when this league was disbanded, they joined the Nottinghamshire League which was later renamed the East Midlands Ladies League. In 1983, they became members of the Women's Premier League. They took the name Sheffield Wednesday Ladies in 1985 and then subsequently, when the FA created the Axa FA Women's League, Sheffield Wednesday Ladies became founder members and have continued in this League to the current day. In 1994 they successfully gained promotion to the FA Women's Premier League where they competed against the top clubs in the women's game. They are currently in the FA Women's League Northern Division and hope to achieve promotion back to the top level. SWLFC are managed by Christine McCann who joined her home town club from Ilkeston Town in January 2003. She successfully attracted several new players to the club for the 2003/04 season to provide experience to compliment the successful youth policy which has seen several youngsters break into the senior team from the under 16s within the last year. The side

are optimistic of making progress in 2004/5 with McCann again successfully attracting several new players from Women's Premier Division clubs Leeds and Doncaster Rovers Belles. Last Season also saw the Owls make breakthroughs in cup competitions, reaching the fifth round of the Women's FA Cup and the final of the Sheffield and Hallamshire County Cup where they lost 2-4 to their local Yorkshire rivals Doncaster Rovers Belles. WLFC have had many players capped for England at all levels and currently have Sarah Smith and Leanne Severns capped at under 19 and under 16 level for England. They also have a thriving youth policy with teams at under 10, 12, 14 and under 16 levels.

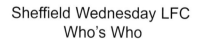

## Sheffield Wednesday LFC Who's Who

**Chairman -** Mark Lalley

**First Team Manger -** Christine McCann

**Physiotherapist** - Helen Lacey

**Secretary -** Ross Padwick

Photographs courtesy of Sheffield Wednesday LFC

SHEFFIELD WEDNESDAY LFC

# History

i n retrospect it was perhaps almost inevitable that Tranmere Rovers, after losing key players to other clubs, would last season be relegated to the Northern Division after eight successful years in the top flight of the Premier League. Louise Edward's young, inexperienced side produced good football during 2003-04 but, was often out-powered by older and bigger opponents. They won just one League match and ended the season bottom of the table. It was a sad, though certainly not irreversible, demise for a club that has been quite a force since its 1990 formation through Football League outfit Tranmere Rovers FCs Football in the Community Scheme. The initial aim was to give local women the opportunity to play football within a structured set-up. Rovers entered the North West Regional League and, after ending their first season as Division Four champions, they simply went on climbing. They won Division One to clinch promotion to the Premier League in 1994-95, by which time a junior section had been set up and the benefits were already being felt as younger players stepped up impressively into Tranmere's

senior side. In their debut Premier League season they convincingly won the Northern Division, going through the whole campaign unbeaten, following which two seasons of consolidation in the National Division established them as a top-flight club. Rovers then enjoyed their most successful three seasons, finishing each in fifth place and culminating in a 2000-01 campaign that also saw them reach The FA Premier League Cup Final, where they lost to an Arsenal team which that year did the treble. At the end of the following season Steve Williams, who had been team manager since the club's formation, stepped down to be replaced by

the long-serving Louise Edwards as player-manager. In her first season in charge Edwards saw her team finish a respectable sixth in the table despite the start of player departures that in 2003-04 were to prove fatal to Rover's National Division status. A tortuous season was set in motion on the opening day, when a 9-2 defeat was suffered at the hands of Arsenal, and there was little respite save for a morale-boosting win against neighbours Everton in October. Some success was enjoyed in the knock-out competitions, especially a 7-1 hammering of Southern Division Watford in the First Round of the Premier League Cup, although Tranmere went out in the following round to Doncaster Rovers Belles. They reached the quarter-finals of The FA Cup, where they lost narrowly to Birmingham City, but they ended the League campaign badly with 8-0 and 7-2 defeats by Fulham and Leeds respectively. More players were lost during last summer's close-

season, but with the club's Centre of Excellence still proving a fruitful source of supply, the 2004-05 season has seen Tranmere blooding a number of youngsters alongside the few seasoned players who have stayed with the Club. Although they have struggled to quickly adapt to the Northern Division, and even though the performances have been good, results have gone against them, Tranmere again reached the quarter finals of the Women's FA Cup before going out to Premier League side Bristol Rovers. Consolidation of their League status has always been the aim this season, with a view to building a squad capable of challenging for promotion back to the top flight in the next few campaigns.

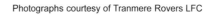

Photographs courtesy of Tranmere Rovers LFC

## Tranmere Rovers LFC Who's Who

**Chairman** - Steve Williams
**Team Manager/Club Secretary** - Louise Edwards
**Assistant Manager** - Shirley Waring
**Physiotherapist** - Dave Charles

TRANMERE ROVERS LFC

# History

*f*ormed in the mid 1970s, Wolverhampton Wanderers Women's FC has risen from modest beginnings to become one of the Midlands top teams. Initially known as Heathfield Rovers they commenced life in the Second Division of the West Midlands League in 1975-76. The name soon changed as they became Wolverhampton and Wednesbury Tube LFC for the next season. This adjustment brought instant rewards as they finished runners-up and were promoted to Division One. The progress continued as they established themselves in the higher level and actually reached the last sixteen of the WFA Cup in 1977-78. The suffix was subsequently dropped and they simply became Wolverhampton Ladies before a backward step was taken in 1983 as they were relegated back to the lower division. Rebuilding took place and Wolves returned to Division One in 1989, this time as champions. The success continued and they finished Division One runners-up the following season. This progress was recognised nationally and Wolves were invited to join the newly formed WFA National League that began in 1991. This exciting new challenge was met head-on, with Wolves finishing in mid table in that initial season in Division One North, and repeating it the following term. The 1993-94 season proved to be a momentous one. Prior to the start of the campaign, the team approached their famous locals asking for permission to use the name Wolverhampton Wanderers Women's FC . Agreement was forthcoming and the name change took place as the team became associated with its Molineux neighbours. The season also proved to be Wolves' most successful as they won the National League Division One North, and with it promotion to the Premier Division. Unfortunately the strength of the club was not good enough and after two seasons they were relegated back to the Northern Division. Since that time the club has consolidated and built on the strength of its youth scheme. The club now has a

wealth of talent at junior level with teams at under 10, 12, 14 and 16 levels, providing the first team with a regular supply of young talent. This has shone through in the last few seasons with a number of players being selected for England at under 17, under 19 and under 21 levels, as well as Emily Westwood now playing for the senior squad. The last three seasons have been fairly successful for Wolves, with challenges being mounted for the League Championship while the Birmingham County Cup has been won twice. Further cup success came in 1999-2000 when the team were within an ace of making the WFA Cup semi-finals, Leeds defeating them in the last quarter of an hour in front of a Noose Lane crowd in excess of five hundred. In October 1999 Wolves Women were incorporated under the Companies Act 1985 as a private company with several influential local business people joining the board including BBC presenter Jenny Wilkes, former England Women's cricket captain Rachel Heyhoe Flint and Managing Director of hygiene supplies company J.Bishop and Co., Roger Morgan. Season 2001-02 saw Wolves Women appoint former Aston Villa European Cup winning captian Dennis Mortimer as manager and he guided them to the runners-up spot in the Northern Division at the first attempt. It was hoped the club would build on this achievement but promotion has eluded them in the following two terms and Dennis stood down at the end of last season due to work commitments. The 2004/05 season has seen the appointment of Paul Taylor, already a well-known figure at the club in his role as physio. With a strong young squad, aided by a few mature players, Paul is already having a significant impact on developing the team.

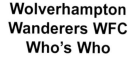

**Wolverhampton Wanderers WFC Who's Who**

**Chairperson** - Jenny Wilkes
**Manager** - Paul Taylor
**Assistant Manager** - Anne Blackham
**Coach** - Dave Ball
**Physio** - Paul Taylor

# The Southern Division

- Brighton & Hove Albion WFC
- Cardiff City LFC
- Chelsea LFC
- Crystal Palace LFC
- Enfield Town LFC
- Ipswich Town WFC
- Langford LFC
- Millwall Lionesses FC
- Portsmouth LFC
- Southampton Saints WFC
- Watford LFC
- Wimbledon LFC

# History

Our Club is called the Brighton & Hove Albion Women and Girls Football Club, and is affiliated to the Sussex County Football Association. The club was formed in 1967 and was known as the GPO Ladies as the majority of players were telephonists. Later they changed their name to C&C Sports following a sponsorship deal with a local sports shop. In 1990 the club was invited to become part of Brighton & Hove Albion FC through its Football in the Community Scheme and changed its name accordingly. The new millennium brought about new changes for us, the support of the professional men's club has been instrumental in our success and we can boast one of the best facilities in the League.

Over the last two seasons we have developed a strong and experienced Management Committee led by BHA Chief Executive Martin Perry. Additional we have established a professional and qualified team of experienced managers and coaches and strengthened all of our squads. We provide playing opportunities to all age groups and have five junior teams and three senior teams. On the

development side, the Centre of Excellence will be entering their third season in the COE League and the Academy at Worthing College will enter its fourth year. We have recently achieved the FA Charter Development Club Award and FA Tops Community Club. This year we have formed a partnership with the Brighton Rugby Club to provide an all year round training facility on grass with the promise of an all weather surface to follow in the coming year. This will enable us to further our aim of providing high standards and quality provision of football to all girls & women and establish ourselves as one of the leading clubs of the South.

Brighton & Hove
Albion WFC
Who's Who

**Chairman -** Martin Perry
**Manager -** Henry Millington
**Physiotherapist -** Becky Fry
**Match and Fixture**
**Secretary** - Brian Shaclock
**Secretary** - David Steer

# History

Cardiff City Ladies football club began life in 1975 when a group of girls got together for a local charity match and realised they had a common love for the sport of football. Just six years later they were the first team to take the All England Five-a-side trophy outside of England. In 1993, Cardiff were finalists in the inaugural Welsh Women's Cup held at The National Stadium. Cardiff were finalists for

established and biggest club in Wales, Cardiff City Ladies Football Club are very proud of their history and present. They are a club providing for the future with opportunities for girls and women of all ages and abilities to participate in the same game of football loved by that group of girls from Llanederyn back in 1975. Most inspirational player Caroline Cooper is captain and midfield Caroline shows her commitment to the CCLFC cause by travelling from Newcastle Emlyn in West Wales to Cardiff each week to play. She came from a small club to further her international ambition with Wales. Since joining Cardiff, Caroline has been a regular in the Wales senior team and collected more than three caps. She is one of two players in the squad who were involved in Cardiff's last campaign in the Premier League back in 2000/01. A tenacious, versatile and influential player who is happy either in defence or midfield, she was voted the management player of the year last season. She is the only player in the squad to make over one hundred first team appearances.

## Cardiff City LFC Who's Who

**Chairman -** Kath Kavanagh

**Manager -** Michelle Adams

**Assistant Manager and Secretary** Karen Jones

three years running before they took home the trophy as Champions. More recently Cardiff City Ladies have been unbeaten in the Welsh Cup for three seasons; being reigning Champions for the last two seasons and getting through to the Semi-Final. Winning the Welsh Cup now brings with it entry into the UEFA Championships, allowing Cardiff to have played international club football in Poland and Croatia against the best club teams from all over Europe. Cardiff have also won the League Cup in 2001 when playing in the South West Combination League. In 1999, Cardiff won this League and again in 2003/2004, this time with a 100% winning record - the first in the League's history - regaining status in the National League. Over the years the club has provided many Welsh International players, often providing half the National Team. There are currently over ten players representing Wales in various age groups including the full senior squad. As the longest

# Season Overview

*t*he season got off to a flyer even before a football had been kicked, when on Wednesday 26th May 2004, George Michaelas announced at the AGM that Chelsea Ladies Football Club had been made an official product of Chelsea Football Club. Chelsea Football in the Community now directs the Women's teams, with George Michaelas maintaining his role as first team manager, and he would lead the push for promotion this season, with the senior side being somewhat more inde-

pendent. Chelsea Ladies kept their home ground, Hampton & Richmond BFC for the forthcoming season, but moved training to the developing men's training ground at Cobham and all-weather training at Feltham Community School. In her first season (03/04), Laura Cooper won both Player's Player and Manager's Player of the Season Awards, and was rightly handed the captaincy for the forthcoming season. Even Laura's parents won an award -- Supporters of the Year. Phil and Sheila Cooper travelled from Sheffield for every Sunday fixture without fail to watch and support Chelsea Ladies; they even travelled to mid-week evening fixtures, taking days off work to support us. Amber

Cook received the Most Improved Player Award, Nicki Dela Salle won the Trevor Parker Award, Nina Downham received the Club Golden Boot for the season, Chairman Robert Regali won a special award for Services to the Club (ten years), plus supporters Roger, Dan, Karen and Andy won special recognition awards for their support to the club. In pre-season, Chelsea Ladies made a number of key signings for the season, with a number of them coming from National Premiership sides: Kyproulla Loizou 'Kyp' was signed from premiership side Charlton Athletic and was the first girl of Greek origin to play for England when she was capped at u18 level. Loizou's partnership with Karen Hills was the foundation of the Charlton defence during 2001/02 and she made twenty one

league and cup appearances. And although the arrival of Casey Stoney and Eartha Pond provided extra competition for places in the following season, she still played eighteen times for Charlton during 2002/03. Another defender was signed, Chelsey Leighton, but this time from Arsenal, another Premiership side, and with her came young goalkeeper Freya Lees from the North Londoners. Chelsea also signed the highly rated and sought after Leanne Small from Watford LFC. The play-maker was an integral part of the Watford side in the previous season and did raise a few eyebrows with some spectacular goals and performances for Watford. Another signing was Lisa Langrish from Portsmouth LFC. Lisa is a natural goal scorer with plenty of premiership experience. As it currently stands, Lisa has scored an amazing seventeen goals in ten games.

Caroline Collie, the regular u21 Scotland Goalkeeper [now pushing for a National team place] was signed mid-season, as was defender Georgie Adams from Premiership side Birmingham, Charlie Nicholson from rivals Langford LFC and Georgie Hoban from the impressive Portsmouth LFC.

## Iceland Tour

Chelsea Ladies did not have a regular pre-season, they went on an all expenses paid tour to Iceland. On Thursday 15th July 2004, a party of twenty three travelled by Iceland Express to Reykjavik to play two matches as a promotion for a tournament hosted by the Icelandic Club, Breidablik FC, which is the home town club of Chelsea striker Eider Gud-johnsen. After being met at the airport by organiser and director of Breida-blik, Benni, and the president of the Chelsea Supporters Club of Iceland, Karl, the girls were whisked away for a late supper and off to bed at midnight, although it was still daylight! Morning training was followed by a visit from the British Ambassador to Iceland and by an evening game in front of over one thousand supporters, mainly Chelsea fans, against Breidablik Ladies. After going a goal behind, the Blues struck back just before the break with a superb strike by new team Captain Laura Cooper. The second half was all one way with the Londoners hitting three goals without reply from Nina

Downham and two from Sam Jones, to cap an impressive performance. The following day the group where taken on a tour of the beautiful sights of a truly wonderful country, visiting the National Park, the amazing spurting Geysers and the breath taking waterfalls. In the evening we were the guests of honours at a dinner and the players and management were asked to do some autograph-signing for the supporters. Three and half hours later and with over four thousand photos signed the team retired with wrist exhaustion! The following day, the girls played their second and final game against a select Iceland National side, which consisted of seven full internationals, five under twenty ones and four under nineteens. Within four minutes the were again 1-0 down, but it got worse ten minutes on when the experienced internationals took a 2-0 lead. But to the girls credit they never stopped believing and by half time the scores were level with two great individual goals by the ever-improving Nina Downham. Nina completed her hat-trick early in the second half, and when Leanne Small struck a volley over the keeper from twenty two yards it looked all over. But a red card for Nicki de la Salle with twenty minutes to go gave the Icelanders hope and when they reduced the deficit to 4-3 it was backs to the wall for the last ten minutes. But credit to all the squad for holding out to record a truly historic win for a club side against a strong National team. Finally before taking our flight home on the Monday, the girls visited the famous Blue Lagoon for a swim in another one of Mother Nature's wonderful mysteries in Iceland.

### Chelsea LFC
### Who's Who

**Chairman** - Robert Regali
**Director of Football** - George Michaelas
**Assistant Manager** - Graham Parker
**Reserve Team Manager** - Mark Callaghan
**Physiotherapist** - Glenn Parker

# History

Crystal Palace Ladies will enter its tenth year in 2005 and 2003/4 was the clubs most successful season to date. The teams from u11s all the way to the seniors all competed in major cup finals and in an amazing week the club took part in five cup finals in seven days. The u 11 won the treble under the guidance of Keith Ingram and were unbeaten for the whole season. The u14s playing against girls eighteen months older competed way above expectations to win the league cup while the u 15s continued their yearly domination of Kent football by winning the league and cup double. The reserves finished both second in the League and runners - up in the League cup while the first team won the South East combination with a twenty one match-winning run to win back to back promotions. The first team also reached a club record of the FA Cup fourth round and were League Cup runners up. The 2004/5 season is looking to be as successful with the seniors now competing in the F.A Premier League which makes the club one of the elite thirty four clubs in the country. The club's plans for the future are to continue the youth development programme and gain the FA Charter Standard Award. Success right across the club has been outstanding and youth development is the most important aspect of the club, as we look to produce players good enough to play first team football at Premier League level. Senior management are two years into a five year plan of reaching the National Premier league and with two back to back promotions in that time, the club is making giant strides towards their goal. The club has the youngest manager in the FA Premier League and is the only team competing at this level

for the first time in its history. These are facts that make the club proud and the ambition and belief in young players and coaches is the key behind the club's success in the past few seasons.

**Crystal Palace LFC
Who's Who**

**Chairman -** Lee Snashfold
**First Team Manager-**
Michael Beale
**Club Physio -**
Andre Vincent

# History

nfield Town Ladies Football Club was founded in 1985 as Merryhills Midgets, a name taken from the primary school that the Founder members attended. The original idea for the club was started when some girls showed an interest in playing football and their parents decided to help them achieve their wish. Two of the founder members, Emma Meads and Melissa Van Gucci, still play within the club. Emma's mum Brenda Abbott is our Honorary President. The club only competed in five-a-side tournaments in the early years, but continued to grow as more players joined. The club has always attempted to provide football for as many players as we can accommodate. This is still the aim of the club today. We are very much a community club, providing training and where possible games for as many players as possible at all levels up to the highest level. The first real success for the club came in the now sadly defunct Metropolitan Police five-a-side tournament where we reached the finals, which ended with a memorable night at Wembley Arena, and then the semi-finals in successive seasons. As the original players became older we decided to join the Eastern Region League in 1989/90, for our first season of eleven a-side football. We were promoted to Division One in our first season. After three years of traveling to Norwich and back several times a season it was decided to enter The Greater London Women's Regional Football League in 1992/93. We were slotted straight into division One. In 1997/98, we gained promotion to the newly formed FA South East Combination League. In our first season we finished seventh, this was followed with third, then runners up and finally in season 2001/02. We were crowned champions and promoted to The FA Premier League, Southern Division.

# Season Overview

he cup was retained the following season, but unfortunately due *to* other circumstances we were unable to complete a hat trick of wins. Some of our younger sides have also won the Middlesex Cup for their age group including the under 11s and under 13s. Over the past few seasons we have fielded sides at senior level (firsts, reserves and thirds) and junior level (under 11s, 12s, 13s and 15s) and have witnessed club membership growing from the original five to well over the hundred mark and is still growing. We are hoping to continue to progress and have more success in the years ahead and to aid this during the summer of 2003 we formed an alliance with the newly formed Enfield Town, after many happy years of being affiliated to Enfield FC. We did this to raise our profile in the home Borough and to assist with the coaching of as many young girls and boys in the local community as possible, and to aid both clubs development and ambition of having a ground of our own within the Borough for men's and women's football. The agreement sees us share the facilities at Brimsdown Sports and Social Club with the hosts own Brimsdown Rovers and Enfield Town Men's sides. To reflect this collaboration the club name was changed to Enfield Town Ladies. Season 2003/04 was a struggle with injuries affecting an already small first team squad and League survival only being guaranteed with a tense final day draw with Merthyr Tydfil that saw them go down instead, along with local rivals Barnet. The under 13s again won the Middlesex cup. The Town match programme was voted best in the country by the Wirral Programme club. After two seasons of relegation struggle the last thing that the club needed was to lose two of its regular defence, but that is what happened with Karen Moss and Kerrie Marlborough for different reasons. Also absent from last season were experienced forward Mel Van Gucci and mid-fielder Bev Payne, so another hard season looked on the cards. A couple of close defeats started the season, when with a little bit of luck, the results could have provided the points the performances deserved. The first point of the season could so easily have been three as two penalties were missed at Portsmouth. The worst performance of the year ended with a defeat at Watford that could have been heavier. The only victory of the season came

in the home game with fellow strugglers Ipswich Town but despite being fairly competitive on the pitch only a couple of draws were gained as the victory was not built on. Before Christmas, the team slipped out of the FA Cup courtesy of a defeat away to QPR. This left only pride to play for as relegation seemed to be certain already. A big win over Hendon in the Middlesex Cup restored confidence to the side and despite remaining unbeaten after Christmas, the damage had already been done and relegation was soon confirmed. With the club forming a closer link with the men's side, that was started to bring senior men's football back to the Borough, the hope is for a far healthier future. A rapid return to the higher level with a stronger team better equipped to cope with the improved standard and the ability to prosper at that level is the dream. The lease at Brimsdown Sports and Social that has been agreed for both the men's and women's team to share with the host club gives us a stable foundation to build on.

## Enfield Town LFC Who's Who

**Chairperson -**
Stacy Russell
**Club Coach -**
John Knight
**Physiotherapist -**
John Abbott
**First Team Manager -**
George Norman

IPSWICH TOWN WFC

# History

*i*pswich Town Women's Football Club was founded in 1985 and joined the East Anglian League reaching the League Cup Final in the opening season. The Reserve team was founded the following year and the First Team achieved the League and Cup double.

In 1989 ITWFC reached the quarter-finals of the Women's FA Cup, a feat that was repeated again in the 1990, 1991 and 1992 seasons. Finishing the top team in the Eastern Region in 1991/2 earned the club a place in the Premier Division of the Women's National League in its inaugural season. We remained in this division for the next season but were relegated to the Northern Division in 1993/4. It was at this point a Youth Section was formed with an Under 14 team. Nurturing the Youth Section has since become a major club strategy to ensure supply of talented young players and this season we have squads from Under 16s through to Under 11s. During the last four seasons, girls from ITWFC have been invited to attend trials at Under 16, Under 18 and Under 19 levels. Last season our Under 19 elect was Stacey Balaam who is now undertaking a Football Scholarship in the USA. We hope that some of this season's talented girls are also selected. In 1995 the team transferred to the Southern Division of the National League and reached the semi final stage of the Women's FA Cup for the first time. The club has since gone through periods of success and consolidation culminating in 2002/3 as our most successful so far, reaching sec-

ond place in the Premier League, Southern Division following an overall run of seven wins from eight games. 2003/4 was not so successful; changes in players and coaches meant that retaining our place in the Premier League Southern Division was hard. Restructuring and the introduction of new players pre-season mean that in 2004/5 we are now ready and able to push once again towards our goal of promotion in 2005/6, if not before!

Ipswich Town WFC
Who's Who

**Chairlady** - Lesley Bowers

**Manager** - Les Earl

**Physiotherapist** - Simon Menell

**Secretary** - Sally Rushbrook

# History

*t*he present Langford Ladies Club was formed in 1969 as Luton Daytels, by a group of daytime telephonists at the Luton telephone exchange. It was one of the founding members of the then Women's Football Association. Those early years in the Chiltern League were fruitful, as the club won the League and Cup on a number of occasions. Promotion in consecutive seasons ensured the club's passage in 1993 into the elite League of women's football in the UK in the Football Association Women's Premier League. The club currently competes in the Southern Division. Home games are played at Langford FC's Forde Park ground as a result of a solid, long- term, relationship with Langford Football Club. In 1997, the club won the All England five-a-side Championships in Birmingham and the name Langford Ladies FC"was placed firmly on the football map. It currently holds the Bedfordshire County Women's Football Trophy. Since its promotion to the FA Women's Premier League, the club has gone from strength to strength and is proud to be recognized as a club that makes a valuable grass-roots contribution to women's football. Players are drawn from a wide area; with the Southern Regional Football Academies providing many young players. Over the last few years a number of international players have signed for the club and we have helped in the development of young players who are now being included in the England National squads at various levels. The young coaching staff are all qualified coaches - some holding UEFA B status, with ambitions to progress further in their line of work. The club is actively working with Langford Football Club on a redevelopment project at Forde Park, which will see the addition of a new stand and the old pitch being completely relaid.

## Langford LFC Who's Who

**Chairman:** Peter Greenslade

**Coaches:** Darren Sarll, Claire Tyrell, Andy Day

**First team Manager/Physio:** Roy Dunsford

# Plans **for the Future**

**O**ur plans for 2005/06 include finding a sponsor to provide some funding to allow us to develop the club further. In particular the development of younger players, and to seek the so far elusive promotion to the National Women's Premier League. Langford Ladies FC has always been a club that prides itself on turning out well-trained and disciplined players and in the latter part of the 2004/5 season we have transferred players to Charlton, Liverpool and Chelsea, and although we are always disappointed to lose our top-flight players we know we are contributing to the development of the women's game as a whole and at the highest possible level. Our aim in the future is to develop a wider player base and to establish girls' teams at all age levels to play in local Leagues.

# History

illwall Lionesses Football Club was founded in 1971 and has been one of the stalwarts of the women's game. The club has led the way, becoming the first women's team to affiliate to a professional men's club. The club has been a Pioneer of the "Football in the Community Scheme" that is now common place amongst football but unheard of in the 70s, and without the support of Millwall Football club, especially in the 70s and 80s, the success we have achieved would not have been possible. With numerous teams and players ranging from eight to thirty-something, we have led the way and been very fortunate to remain amongst the top teams in this country. The advancement of the women's game ha s led Millwall Lionesses to become a major player in the "Millwall Community" programme and we now play an active part in the development of girls football in the community.

Millwall were the first club to have a Female Centre of Excellence, which is now common-place with the top women's clubs. Through our youth policy we have developed many talented players who have gone on to gain international honours either with the Lionesses or other clubs. Current players who have gained international honours include Pru Buckley, Amy Mason and Ayo Adetayo. The club this season will be fielding two senior teams. The first team playing in the FA Women's Premier League Southern Division, and the second team in the Southern Premier League Reserve Division 1. Our junior teams will be competing in the South East FA Centre of Excellence League at under 16/14/12 and under 10. We also have a development section for those players who have not yet reached the Centre of Excellence standard. Although the club is in a transition period at the moment, with the exciting developments taking place within our youth policy, we believe the club can once again become a force in women's football.

MILLWALL LIONESSES FC

**Millwall Lionesses FC
Who's who**

**President -** Theo Paphitis
**Chairman -** Arthur Mason
**First Team Player/Manager -** Pru Buckley
**Head Coach -** Jim Hicks
**Physiotherapist -** Christina Sochinachan

133

# History

Portsmouth Football Club Ladies was formed in 1987, with just the bare eleven players. The club entered the Southern Region League in 1988 where they enjoyed ten good seasons. During this period the club started introducing youth teams to compete at local level. In 1998, Portsmouth F.C. Ladies gained promotion into the South West Combination League in its founder season, and the same year saw them win the South West Combination League Cup beating Reading Royals 3-1 in the final In 1998, Portsmouth entered their first Foreign Tournament, travelling to Holland to compete in the Coca Cola 'Harlem Cup'. It was celebrations all round as Portsmouth beat Rigterbleek 1-0 to bring the cup home. 1999 saw Fourteen players and officials take their first steps in coaching by taking the F.A. Junior Team Managers Award. By 2000 Portsmouth F.C. Ladies officially introduced a youth structure within the club, catering for U14 and U12 teams. This has since gone from strength to strength and now the club has eight youth teams competing in various leagues. In 2002, Vanessa Raynbird was appointed as first team Manager and Malcolm Poore as First Team Coach. By 2002 , the club became the first women's club in Hampshire to receive the F.A. Charter Standard Club Award for excellence in provision of coaching and support staff. The club won the South West Combination League in 2002/2003, dropping only two points during the course of the season to gain promotion in to the Premier League Southern Division for the first time in the club's history 2002/2003 also saw Portsmouth F.C. Ladies join ranks with Chichester College to set up an Academy for girls between the age of sixteen and nineteen, where they can continue their academic studies as well as participating in coaching sessions and Academy games on a weekly basis. In 2003/2004 The First Team maintained their status in the Premier League Southern Division and beat Southampton Saints 3-0 in the final of the Hampshire County Women's Cup to win the trophy for the first time in the club's history. The reserves won the Premier League Reserves Southern Division Two to gain promotion in to Division One. Currently Portsmouth F.C. Ladies have a first team playing in the Premier League Southern Division. The reserves are in the Division One South of the Premier League. They have a third team (Portsmouth F.C. Ladies A) playing in Division One of the Southern Regional League. The Youth Section has an u16 team in Division Two of the Hampshire League, two u14 11-a-side teams both of which play in the Hampshire u14 League, an U13 side in the South Hants Glass U13 Small Sided League, three u12 teams in the South Hants Glass u12 small sided League and an u10 team in the Winchester and District Small Sided League. Many players at senior, u18 and u16 level have been selected on a regular basis to play for Hampshire over the past nine years in Competitive Representative Football. 2004/5 Secured Perry's Peugeot of Portsmouth as first team shirt sponsors.

### Portsmouth LFC
### Who's Who

**Chairman**: Thura K. T. Win

**Director of Football:** Steve Friend

**First Team Manager**: Vanessa Raynbird

**First Team Coach**: Malcolm Poore

**First Team Fitness Coach:** Sharon Hayes

# History

*r*ed Star Southampton WFC was formed in 1979, and played in the Home Counties League, and later in the Southern Regions League. In 1991, the team were winners of the Southern Region Division One title and subsequently became one of the founder members of the inaugural Women's National League. Affiliations to Southampton FC came in 1995/96 with Red Star changing its name to Southampton Saints. At the start of the 2001/2002 season, Saints merged with Southampton Football Club with their Chairman Rupert Lowe also becoming chairman of Southampton Saints Women. The women's team receive the same quality of coaching and support afforded to their male counterparts. A reserve team operates in the FAPL Reserve Southern Division. At youth level Southampton FC operates a very successful FA Centre of Excellence.

**SOUTHAMPTON SAINTS WFC**

## Southampton Saints WFC
## Who's Who

**Chairman -** Rupert Lowe

**Manager -** Sue Lopez

**Physiotherapist -** Mo Gimple

**Secretary -** Ros Wheeler-Osman

# History

Watford Ladies in its present form is a combination of Watford Ladies FC and Watford Town Girls FC and the merger has provided an outstanding footballing opportunity for girls and women of all abilities. Watford Ladies FC was formed back in 1970 following a number of letters received by Watford FC to start a ladies section of the supporter's club, whereupon advertisements were circulated for any interested players to attend a meeting. The first meeting took place at Watford Fields Junior School and over forty girls attended. It was agreed to hold trials at Cassiobury Park, and these brought forth a team of eighteen players to be managed by Doug Hewish and coached by John Williams and Mike Walker. The club performed extremely well in its formative years and was fortunate to exist during the early years of organised Ladies League Football. Watford Ladies, under the current management team of Darren Ward and Paul Tarver along with Rick Murphy and Matt Ward, gained promotion to the Women's Premier League in 2003 and finished a creditable fifth in their first season in top-flight football. In 2004, the club achieved Charter Standard Club Status. These honors reflect the club as one of the leading teams in the country.

## The Future

Priority for Watford Ladies is to remain in the top flight of women's football. Running the club is down to people who give up their unpaid time for the love of the game. Watford Ladies are self-funded and get no support from Watford FC. Numerous meetings to gain their support have thus far failed, and like many clubs, fund raising and sponsorship makes it possible for clubs to continue.

Having recently moved to Sun Postal Sports, Watford Ladies can boast one of the best facilities around with a good pitch and newly built changing rooms, all part of Sun Postal's ground development. These facilities are also available to our youth teams who play in local leagues. With all of the support and backing Watford do get, it is our hope that one day we may gain promotion into the National Premier League.

**Watford LFC
Who's who**

**Chairman -** Eric Wood-Thompson

**Vice Chairman -** Cordula Schirmeister

**First Team Managers -** Darren Ward
and Paul Tarver

**Reserve Manager -** Phil Longuehay

# History

AFC Wimbledon Ladies - Unique and Wants to Remain so.

*t*he club started way back in 1974 as Friends of Fulham, later it was affiliated to Wimbledon FC where it grew and grew and at one point had three senior squads and four junior teams - that's over one hundred players, plus a very large sprinkling of parents! However, the junior teams were ushered away from the female club to form the Wimbledon FC female football centre of excellence when shortly thereafter the men's club moved to Milton Keynes and eventually a great deal of interest was to be lost. This also meant the senior female squads faced little financial support from the men's club and despite each player already paying £125 a year as well as their own costs for away games, it left an enormous hole in the accounts. It was then we approached AFC Wimbledon as they had pioneered the wonderful concept of 'self belief' and then, The Dons Trust stepped in, and after some necessary negotiations agreed to finance the female side of the club and from season 2003/4 we were known as AFC Wimbledon Ladies. I'm not blasting a public relations address here! Stay with me - it's important! I want to repeat we have the full backing of our sponsors and our club -- that to a degree is unusual for many female clubs. Yes it is! Many are given a 'pepper corn' contribution by their associated men's club - to be seen as doing the right thing - very PC. But if the sponsors' interest ends there, then the development of the game ends there! I mentioned in the title we are unique, and hope this becomes apparent. We provide probably the best playing as well as training facilities in our league. We set a standard to which other female clubs would love to aspire. Yes, it sounds patronising, but it's true and it's a good thing! Not least for our players but - as importantly - for the female game. It gives a level to which many other female clubs want to aspire. It's all very easy to bemoan one's lot and it's a difficult situation to rattle once the rot has set in. Nowadays, girls expect a great deal from a club - not just football. Let's take a look at what the average club should offer; adequate pitch, proper training, changing room facilities, kit (home and away), coaches and physio, and the rest. As a Premier League Football Club AFC Wimbledon Ladies provide a four thousand capacity stadium, two enormous heated changing rooms with showers, superb training facilities twice a week, hospitality for visiting teams of the highest order, superb home/away and training kits as well as tracksuits and bags. It also provides FIFA coaches and physio, in addition to transport to away games, as well as the best match day programme in the League and all this costs the players nothing. And in today's game, it's imperative to have good lines of communication and thus we have a fantastic dedicated web site, updated regularly - please visit www.afcwl.co.uk

## We're Lucky - and We Know It!

*a*s mentioned earlier, we are lucky and yes we know it, but this did not come about by simply wishing, hoping and occasional moaning. No, this came about through hard work of a committee - not just one person doing everything but a group of dedicated people who work tirelessly to provide, maintain and develop the facilities at AFC Wimbledon. Equally, we are developing a programme to enable us to get into the National Premier League. We realise we need to nurture a team that will not only achieve National League status but also has the ability plus inner strength to remain there. It's all very well to gain promotion - retaining it is a very difficult job indeed. Fortunately we have the wonderful Wimbledon spirit here at the club, which captures everyone - players, supporters and members equally! But we're not blind to reality - there are other very good clubs in our League and we have had a 'stop start' season. We are currently in the higher echelons of the table but it's fair to recognise the strength of other teams and the possibility of finishing lower than top three. However, we will learn by this, then next season will be a different scenario, which is the whole point of running a club at this level - learn, accept and develop. And remember, no one hands you everything you want - you have to win - on and off the pitch. So, "come on you Dons!"

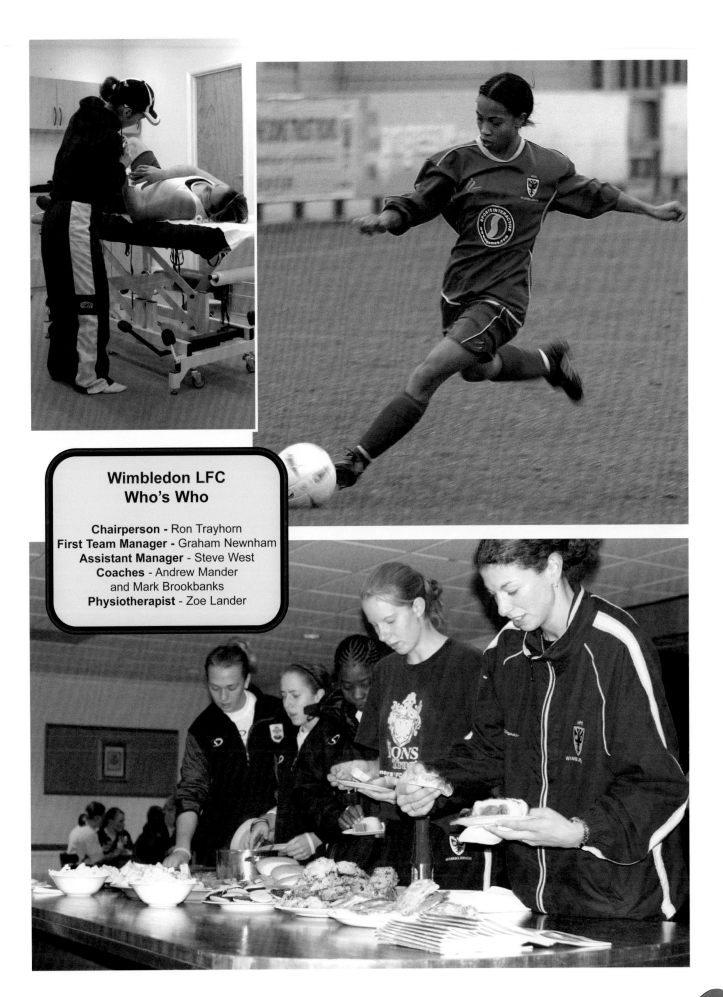

**Wimbledon LFC
Who's Who**

**Chairperson -** Ron Trayhorn
**First Team Manager -** Graham Newnham
**Assistant Manager -** Steve West
**Coaches -** Andrew Mander
and Mark Brookbanks
**Physiotherapist -** Zoe Lander

# List of County F.As

**Amateur Football Alliance**
Website: www.amateur-fa.com
Email : info@amateur-fa.com

**Army FA**
Website: www.armyfa.co.uk
Email: info@armyfa.com

**Bedfordshire FA**
website: www.bedfordshirefa.com
Email: info@bedfordshirefa.com

**Berks and Bucks FA**
Website: www.berksandbucksfa.com
Email: info@berks-bucksfa.com

**Birmingham FA**
Website: www.bcfa.co.uk
Email: info@birmingham.com

**Cambridgeshire FA**
Website:www.cambridgeshirefa.com
Email: info@cambridgeshirefa.com

**Cheshire FA**
Website: www.cheshirefa.com
Email: info@cheshirefa.com

**Cornwall FA**
Website:www.cornwallfa.com
Email:secretary@cornwallfa.com

**Cumberland FA**
Website: www.cumberlandfa.com
Email: secretary@cumberlandfa.com

**Derbyshire FA**
Email: info@derbyshirefa.com

**Devon FA**
Website: www.devonfa.com
Email: info@devonfa.com

**Dorset FA**
Website:www.dorsetfa.com
Email:footballoperations@dorsetfa.com

**Durham FA**
Email: john.topping@durhamfa.com

**East Riding FA**
Website: www.eastridingfa.com
Email: info@eastridingfa.com

**English Schools FA**
Website: www.esfa.co.uk
Email: info@schoolsfa.com

**Essex FA**
Website: www.essexfa.com
Email: info@essexfa.com

**Gloucestershire FA**
Website: www.gloucestershirefa.com
Email: info@gloucestershirefa.com

**Guernsey FA**
Website: www.guernseyfa.com
Email:matt.fallaize@guernseyfa.com

**Hampshire FA**
Website: www.hampshirefa.com
Email: info@hampshirefa.com

**Herefordshire FA**
Email:val.lambert@herefordshirefa.com

**Hertfordshire FA**
Website: www.hertfordshirefa.com
Email: secretary@hertfordshirefa.com

**Huntingdon FA**
Website: www.huntsfa.com
Email: info@huntsfa.com

**Isle Of Man FA**
Email: ann.garrett@isleofmanfa.com

**Jersey FA**
Website: www.jerseyfa.com
Email: gill.morgan@jerseyfa.com

**Kent FA**
Email: paul.dolan@kentfa.com

**Lancashire FA**
Website: www.lancashirefa.com
Email: secretarylancashirefa.com

**Leicestershire FA**
Email: info@leicestershirefa.com

**Lincolnshire FA**
Website: www.lincolnshirefa.com
Email: secretary@lincolnshirefa.com

**Liverpool FA**
Website: liverpoolfa.com
Email: secretary@liverpoolfa.com

**London FA**
Website: www.londonfa.com
Email: info@londonfa.com

**Manchester FA**
Website: www.manchesterfa.com
Email: info@manchesterfa.com

**Middlesex FA**
Website: www.middlesexfa.com
Email: info@middlesexfa.com

**Norfolk FA**
Website: www.norfolkfa.com
Email: info@norfolkfa.com

**Northamptonshire FA**
Email:
d.payne@northamptonshirefa.com

**North Riding FA**
Website: www.northridingfa.com
Email: info@northridingfa.com

**Northumberland FA**
Email:
rowland.maughan@northumberland-fa.com

**Nottinghamshire FA**
Website:www.nottinghamshirefa.com
Email: info@nottinghamshirefa.com

**Oxfordshire FA**
Website: www.oxfordshirefa.com
Email: info@oxfordshirefa.com

**RAF FA**
Website: www.mod.uk/raffa
Email:
satco@direct.shawburyigs.raf.mod.uk

**Royal Navy FA**
Website: www.royalnavyfa.com
Email: secretary@navyfa.com

**Sheffield and Hallamshire FA**
Website: www.sheffieldfa.com
Email: info@sheffieldfa.com

**Shropshire FA**
Email: secretary@shropshirefa.com

**Somerset FA**
Email: info@somersetfa.com

**Staffordshire FA**
Email:secretary@staffordshirefa.com

**Suffolk FA**
Website:www.suffolkfa.com
Email:info@suffolkfa.com

**Surrey FA**
Website:www.surreyfa.com
Email:info@surreyfa.com

**Sussex FA**
Website:www.sussexfa.com
Email:info@sussexfa.com

**Westmorland FA**
Website:www.westmorlandfa.com
Email:info@westmorlandfa.com

**West Riding FA**
Website:www.wrcfa.com
Email:info@wrcfa.com

**Wiltshire FA**
Email:mike.benson@wiltshirefa.com

**Worcestershire FA**
Website:www.worcestershirefa.com
Email:info@worcestershirefa.com

*Charlton Athletic Ladies-
2005 FA Cup Winners*

THE FA NATIO